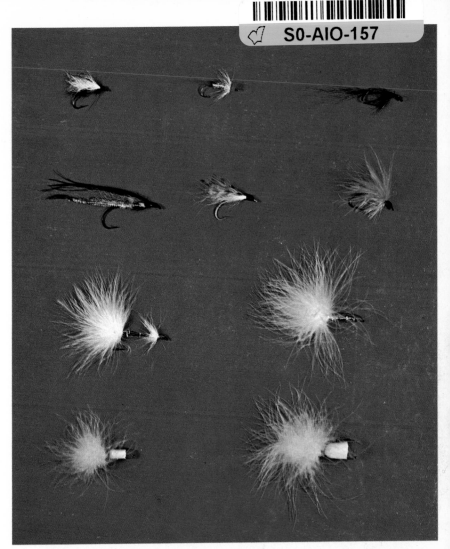

Flies and poppers. *Top row, left to right:* A size 6 Royal Coachman, a size 6 Carl Ludemann shad fly, and a size 4 Smith River salmon fly. *Second row:* A size 1/0 Humboldt Bay, California, anchovy type fly for salmon, a Hagen Sands bonefish fly, and a pink streamer pattern tied for bonefish on sizes 1/0 and 4 hooks, respectively. *Third row:* A size 2, 3 extra-long hook marabou streamer fly (two patterns) used for most ocean-going fish. *Fourth row:* A size 6 popper (a 2-inch baby) and a size 2 popper. The hook is a 3 extra-long regular-weight wire, "S" hump, ringed eye. The size 2 popper is about 3¼ inches overall.

Salt-Water Fly-Fishing
HANDBOOK
by Sam Nix

1973
DOUBLEDAY & COMPANY, INC.
GARDEN CITY, NEW YORK

The book is dedicated to S. Arthur Love, Jr., of Norwood, Pennsylvania. His help and encouragement were indispensable.

ISBN: 0-385-04033-4
Library of Congress Catalog Card Number 71–180095

1

Contents

ACKNOWLEDGMENTS

THE BIG TEN (Alphabetically)

Harlon Bartlett, San Diego *Evening Tribune* outdoor writer, who assisted in putting the finishing touches on the book

Angus Cameron, Vice President and Senior Editor of Alfred A. Knopf

Phillip Clock, President of Fenwick/Sevenstrand

Dr. Albert C. Funk, a great all-around salt-water fly man

Jim Green, Production Manager of Fenwick/Sevenstrand

Myron Gregory, casting and fishing expert

George Herrick, former San Diego *Evening Tribune* outdoor writer

Leon Martuch, President of Scientific Anglers, Inc.

Stewart Richardson, Editor in chief of Doubleday & Company

Rolla Williams, San Diego *Union* outdoor writer

THE JUNIOR SET (Teen-agers)

Bud Crist, fishing companion; Chris Crowson, amateur fly tier; Jeff Crowson, amateur photographer; Mike Sands, Florida Keys fishing expert; and Jimmy White, a dedicated fly fisherman.

AND OTHERS

Roberto Balderrama, Bryce Dabler, Enrique Fitch Diaz, Charles "Chuck" Elget, Irv and Alva Elliott, Carol and Sandy Green, Frank Lawrence, J. Stanley Lloyd, Carl Ludemann, Pat and Art Parks, Harlan and Mary Ann Price, Chester "Champ" Richards, Hagen Sands, Bill Schaadt, Anita Schenk, Fred Schrier, Fred and Fredric Smittle, George Stewart, Jr., E. J. Strickland, Ted Trueblood, and Hugh Wright Turner.

FLY AND TACKLE COMPANIES

Scientific Anglers Inc., Midland, Michigan
Fenwick/Sevenstrand, Westminster, California
Mason Tackle Company, Otisville, Michigan
Lamiglas Corporation, Kent, Washington
Dupont's Plastic Department, Wilmington, Delaware
Stewart's Tackle Shop, Coos Bay, Oregon
Buz's Fly and Tackle Shop, Visalia, California
Black's Custom Flies, Roseburg, Oregon
Butler's Fly and Tackle Shop, Santa Rosa, California
International Hook Company, Denver, Colorado
Eagle Claw-Wright and McGill Company, Denver, Colorado
Tucker Duck and Rubber Company, Ft. Smith, Arkansas
And the following San Diego dealers: Rod and Stream, Perry's
Sport Store, and Midway Bait and Tackle Company

Introduction

When one speaks of fly fishing in salt water, the meaning is perfectly clear. But what is salt-water fly fishing? Tarpon and snook come from the salt water and enter fresh water rivers. If they are classified as salt-water fish (and they are so classified), how can we omit shad, salmon, and steelhead? Their habits in this respect are identical. Fishing in the ocean with a fly rod is a fairly new sport, but fly fishing for the above-named fish is an old sport. I caught my first steelhead 40 years ago, and fly men were catching steelhead in Oregon's Rogue River as early as 1912. Fly fishing in the Gulf of California (the Sea of Cortez) goes back to 1962, so we can consider that type of fishing fairly new.

This book covers any fish that has had a good taste of salt water and has been part of my experience of successful fishing for more than 25 varieties of salt-water game fish. Most of the action takes place along the California coast, the Oregon coast, and in the Gulf of California. The instructive information will be of great value to the newcomer to the sport and will be of interest to the more advanced student.

My first experience with the ocean-going fish took place years ago in California's mighty Klamath River. A fish hit my Royal Coachman and raced down the strong current with my Hardy St. John reel screaming. I finally beached my first steelhead, the fish that turned me into a tramp—a fishing tramp.

In the early 1950s, the word went out on shad fishing in the Russian, American, Feather, and Yuba rivers of California. The fly men responded. Great numbers of these fish are hooked, landed, and released. This fishing is so exciting that I have missed only two seasons in the last sixteen.

I pioneered fly fishing along the accessible beaches of approximately three hundred miles of Mexico's shoreline. Sierra mackerel, corvina, ladyfish, pampano, and other fish came to my popping bugs. Jacks and bass hit the streamers.

Salmon, striped bass, bonito, yellowtail, and albacore are available to the fly man. These fish are caught along the West Coast.

On trips covering approximately 25,000 miles, I learned how to fish for bonefish, tarpon, snook, and other fish of southern Florida. These fish deserve their high rating, and I look back on that fishing with the greatest of pleasure.

Salt-Water Fly-Fishing
HANDBOOK

CHAPTER 1

Casting Pools and Fly-Fishing Clubs

Casting pools have been in existence for many years and were used, primarily, by tournament casters. These experts have, through years of trial-and-error effort, brought distance casting within the range of the every-day fly rodder. Too many present-day fishermen, especially beginners, either ignore the benefits offered by casting pools or are not aware of them. A casting pool is the place for the beginner to learn the first principles of casting as well as the place for the more advanced student to become an expert with practice and more practice.

It is not necessary to be a world-champion caster to be successful on fishing trips, but casting ability will certainly help. At times, success does depend upon the ability to cast a long line— to get that fly out into the productive water.

The newcomer should make the correct approach to casting by going to a pool get-together—usually a Sunday morning event—before looking in the Yellow Pages for the location of the nearest tackle shop. Excellent instructors with good practice outfits are available at these meetings, and both are free for the asking. The instructors are dedicated fly men and are glad to help anyone interested in this important first phase of fly fishing.

The following tackle has been carefully selected for teaching purposes—and teaching purposes only—in an economical way and a suitable way. It does the job. Eight and one-half feet is the ideal rod length, and it can be assembled from Herters No.

RB6H20 blanks. No. 7 double-tapered lines (30 yards in length) were cut to furnish two 45-foot lengths from each factory line, since 45 feet of line is long enough for teaching purposes. This cuts the line cost in half. Practice lines take a beating and do have to be replaced.

A low-priced reel (for line storage only), a few feet of level leader material, and a small fly with the barb removed—as a safety factor—complete the instructional outfit. The No. 7 line is one or two sizes heavier than would be used for fishing, but the additional weight is needed to bring out the rod's action in the short casts recommended for beginners. Twenty feet of line is enough, since good timing, not distance, is the initial goal.

After the beginner learns to cast a short line, he is then ready for instruction on distance casting—the kind needed in salt-water work. Heavier and longer rods with heavier lines are needed, and these outfits are also available at pool meetings.

In referring to distance casting, we are not concerned with the 200-foot or more casts made by the tournament experts. We are interested in learning to get out 70 to 100 feet of line. However, if I ever made a 100-foot cast while fishing, I would tell somebody about it—a lot of somebodies. The beginner will soon learn that casting-pool distance is easier to get than fishing distance, especially if he is in water up to his elbows (anything deeper is known as skin diving).

When the beginner picks up the heavier outfit, he will notice that the main feature of this new (to him) outfit is the type of line. It is called a Shooting Head and is used with shooting line, which will be discussed later on. This type of line is used by almost all instructors and almost all West Coast fly men for their salt-water fishing. The beginner at distance casting will have to keep his cool, since he will have some problems with the outfit, especially with the monofilament shooting line. But with patience, good instruction, and lots of practice, he will be pleasantly surprised by his long casts. During the practice sessions, he should use as many different long rods as possible to gain an insight on what will suit him for fishing. And when his mind is finally made up, he is making good progress. He becomes "the more advanced student." He is now ready to advance on a tackle salesman. The salesman will enjoy—I hope—the experience of waiting on a fly man who knows what he wants. It saves wear and tear on the crystal ball most salesmen of fly tackle seem to need.

But what if a casting pool cannot be located within what is considered driving distance? If I were just starting out on this casting business, I would not hesitate to drive, say, 100 miles to a pool, realizing, as I do, the advantages—the value of the instructions I would receive when I arrived. Casting can be learned at home, especially with the assistance of a fly-fishing nut, or it can be learned "by the book." But I strongly advise the casting pool method, if at all possible, for the first lesson or two.

Fly-fishing clubs are springing up all over the country, and they are of great service to fly men, especially the newcomers to the game. The less one knows, the greater the benefits. The club meetings are worthwhile, especially meetings that feature rod-making and fly-tying. At times, movies are shown of some yokel catching fish, but it is my humble opinion that these movies are worth little as educational tools for the fly fisherman. Their sole asset is entertainment. These meetings are usually open to the public.

CHAPTER 2

The Fly Line

Looking back on 50 years of fly fishing could give an old-timer some "loose bolts." He now realizes that he knew little about most of his gear and almost nothing about fly lines. Knowledge of the fact that most old-timers were in the same boat will give him a needed wrench. In those days of few fly men and few line companies, there were few sources of information. But show no sympathy for this old boy, since he had it real good in spite of the line situation. Any lack of line knowledge was compensated for by an ample supply of fish—the catching of which was his specialty. So cheer up, old-timer, you were not so dumb, after all.

Line confusion was caused by the marking of lines by diameter without considering the specific gravity of material used in construction. Silk is heavier than nylon and lighter than Dacron, and since rod action is related to weight and not diameter, the reason for the confusion is clear.

A few years ago, a committee composed of several dedicated fly men decided that they had "had it" with the old confusing system. They came up with a new system—describing lines by weight only, the weight to be based on the first 30 feet of line, excluding the two feet or so of level tip-section. All fly fishermen owe those "brains" a lot of thanks and several *olés*.

Here are the *present standards* for the lines suitable to salt-water fishing:

		Minus-Plus
Line Number	Weight in Grains	Tolerances
9	240	230–50
10	280	270–90
11	330	318–42

The avoirdupois standard of 437.5 grains to the ounce is used. Only two types of lines are practical for this fishing:

The **WEIGHT-FORWARD TAPERED LINE** (for descriptive purposes only) has 2 feet of level tip section, 10 feet of front taper, 18 feet of heavy (belly) line, 3 feet of back taper, and 57 feet of small shooting line for the over-all standard length of 30 yards.

This type is said to be popular on the East Coast, but it is seldom used by West Coast anglers. I find little use for it. It has its place for some phases of bonefishing—for us old fogies who can, maybe, see a bonefish as far away as 35 feet. It is not a "shooter," but fair distance can be obtained by false casting. This line takes up a great amount of reel space—space that may be needed for backing line. To gain more space for backing, some of the shooting line can be discarded. Discarding, say, 15 feet would mean about 60 feet of extra backing in the 20-pound class. The amount to cut depends upon the individual's casting ability (as to distance).

The **SHOOTING HEAD** line. This type of line is also well known as a Shooting Taper. It is a single tapered line, which has (for descriptive purposes only) 2 feet of level tip section, 10 feet of front taper, and 18 feet of heavy (belly) line. It has no back taper. The factory lines have a loop of heavy squidding line at the butt for a connection with the shooting line.

Scientific Anglers, Inc. makes these lines (under the name Shooting Tapers) in the floating and sinking kinds—the latter in slow, fast, and extra-fast (HiD) rates. The HiD is most useful. It should be noted that their No. 10 line weighs 300 grains —an extra-heavy No. 10—but can be specially ordered in 275 grains.

Some anglers prefer less than the factory 30-foot length. Since the tapered part of the line is usually satisfactory, the cutting is done at the butt end. Because each foot of line removed means a reduction in weight of 10 to 14 grains, too much shortening can place the line in a lower category. It may be necessary to start with a line of the next larger size. A short line is easier to pick up from the water than a longer one, and works well from a boat and from a shore with a background that might give trouble with a longer line.

My floating Shooting Heads were made from Scientific Anglers, Inc. large double-tapered lines, before the company marketed Shooting Heads. Originally, the lines were designed for the Hardy Brothers of England, with long tapers for dry fly fishing —English style. The G2AG (old system) makes up into No. 9 heads, and the G3AG is used for No. 10 heads. My method of cutting the line for heads is simple—maybe too simple. I take the factory line and chop off the first 5 feet. This takes care of the level tip section and 3 feet of the long taper—this shortened taper suits me for popper casting. A better but more complicated method would be to cut a 40-foot section from the factory line and test the long taper for proper turnover, using the largest popper you will use in your fishing. By the cut-and-try method, the suitable taper length will be determined. Weigh this section and trim the butt end as required. Each foot of G2AG heavy (belly) line weighs about 9 grains—the G3AG about 12 grains. The needed loop for the shooting line connection will be taken up later on. The floating head is, of course, needed for popper fishing and has the added advantage that the popper can be replaced with a streamer fly for surface-type fish.

At about this point, some reader is no doubt thinking that in order to weigh lines, a scale of some kind is needed. A powder scale is the answer. The one I bought (from Herters) has a capacity of 325 grains, but I would suggest one of 400 grains for weighing the heaviest of lines. The cost of the scale is $11.00, and it will last for years. A scale of this type is indispensable to "Ye Compleat Angler."

A length of level lead-core line is sometimes used as a Shooting Head. The 18-pound test (.028 inch in diameter) weighs approximately 12.5 grains a foot, so a 20-foot length should place it in a No. 9 line classification. The 50-yard spools are low priced, so a "head" can be made up for less than 50 cents. Lead core is miserable material to use and can become a lethal weapon if used under any casting condition—crowded or uncrowded. The line is used on salmon and stripers, especially, since it sinks very fast and cuts through wind with ease, but I know of no one who laughs when using it—not if he wants to keep his pearly white teeth. One of these days, I am going to patent a half-and-half line—half lead core and half regular fly line. It might work very well by keeping the lead core part always out past the rod's tip-top when casting. Self loops are made for the leader and shooting line connections.

The **SHOOTING LINE** is usually limp monofilament in the 20- or 25-pound class. The former has a diameter of about 19/1000—a popular size. Small diameter and smoothness of the material result in long casts. For this reason—and this reason only—monofilament is used by almost 100 percent of the West Coast fly men for salt-water fishing.

Except for the distance feature, the fly man who uses monofilament for this purpose is not riding any gravy train. It does kink at times—usually the wrong time; it is adversely affected by the sun and salt water; it is more wearing on the rod's tip-top and guides than regular fly line, and it is potentially dangerous. If a fish of good size and speed gets into high gear with a coil of monofilament wrapped around one's finger or wrist, something will give way—and that something will be precious skin. What would happen if a coil should get around a fly man's neck during such a battle is too horrible to contemplate. One of our presidents (line company type) has the scars on one of his fingers to prove my point. This is just a warning to be careful when using the stuff. These large and speedy fish should not be passed up because of any potential danger.

Use care in transferring the shooting line from its spool to the fly reel to keep it as kink free as possible. Kinks seem to disappear in the current of rivers but are almost impossible to get rid of in the ocean water. It helps to keep monofilament on large-diameter storage reels when not in use—one of my fishing friends uses an old bicycle wheel. Stretching the material before using helps. Discard the piece (the 75-to-100-foot length) if and when trouble occurs. The cost is low.

Recommending a brand of monofilament for shooting line could be dangerous to my health. It could be meaningless. No two fly men seem to agree on any one brand. What is known as "wide" monofilament (the 20-pound class measures .013 by .030 inch) should be mentioned. It works good until it kinks. But one thing I am sure of: If you learn to live with the stuff, you will stick with it through thick and thin. Monofilament as a shooting line has no equal. I may be overemphasizing the disadvantages.

BACKING LINE is needed on long-running fish and to help fill the spool of the reel to a near maximum capacity, which insures the largest-possible-diameter coils of the monofilament shooting line, which in turn lessens the kink problem.

The amount of backing required for fishing is difficult to determine. Two hundred yards should be sufficient, but you will never know until you are "wiped out." Then you will be out of backing but "in" an almost unbelievable story—the only kind worth telling.

Braided Dacron in the 20-pound class has a diameter of 16/1000, compared to 20/1000 for salt-water squidding line in the same class. This means that a reel that will hold a maximum of 200 yards of 20-pound class Dacron will be filled to capacity with only 130 yards of 20-pound test squidding line. I use 20-pound class as an example, since that is the minimum size I use. With enough reel capacity, I would use a larger size (as a safety factor). Dacron may cost a little more than squidding line, but it is worth more. Both types are durable and give long service. How much backing to use is discussed later under "The Fly Reel."

The diameter and not the pound test of backing, shoot line, and leader material is the working factor—a factor that has been ignored by many fly men and tackle manufacturers. Diameters should be clearly marked on this material, but it seldom is. Pound test does not mean much. If I can get 14 pounds of pull before breaking a piece of 20-pound class material, I am doing well. Mistakes are sometimes made in the marketing of the material. Recently, I "miked" a 100-yard spool of 10 pound test monofilament and one of 12-pound test. They have the same diameter, and I now have 200 yards of 12-pound test, which, used as 24-inch tippets, will last me well into the next century.

Loops and knots to connect the shooting line to the Shooting Head and to the backing will be given later on. A pound-test-to-diameter chart will also be given, in as standard a way as possible.

CHAPTER 3

The Fly Rod

Even if I could consider myself an expert on the subject, I could not select a salt-water-type fly rod for you, the individual. There are just too many factors involved. But I can give you one happy thought: Once the proper selection is made, the rest of the tackle falls into place.

The most important factor to consider is the length of cast needed to get the fly into productive water. My first experience with shad fishing was a failure. The fish were there and were being caught, but I could not cast far enough in that particular riffle to reach the fishy water. I finally caught fish by moving to another riffle where I could reach the productive water. A cast of 80 feet or more is often needed, but that is not so easy when standing up to the elbows in moving water. It requires the combination of casting ability, the correct line, and rod to match the line.

Continuous casting is the rule for this fishing. Bonefishing is an exception, because it is more hunting than casting. Fishing is for fun, so work is to be avoided. Take this under consideration in choosing the line-rod outfit while keeping the need for distance casting in mind.

Rod strength can be ignored, since any rod selected will handle the hooked-up fish we are interested in. Once the fish is hooked it is fought from the reel and by the reel, which takes care of the matter. Rod weight is considered only as it pertains to the weight of the line used. Most rods are in the 5-ounce class, but rod weight does not mean very much, since the rod fittings determine the over-all weight. In my opinion, casting weight of the line is what causes any wear and tear on the fly man.

You won't be casting No. 16 trout flies. Salt-water flies are on the heavy side, especially if weighted with lead wire. This weight does cut down on casting distance.

Strain on the old pocketbook is a factor not only in the rod selection but also with the rest of the necessary equipment.

If my comments are considered, you will at least have something to help keep you on the course—to make rod selection more efficient.

I wish I had considered the factors involved 18 years ago when I was preparing for a 3000-mile trip from my home to the Florida Keys. Instead, I read an article in a fishing magazine. I bought the recommended rod—an expensive split bamboo job—and the recommended line. It turned out to be too much rod, especially since the recommended line was too light in weight. So I used the outfit for one day and then took up one of my other rods—a lighter and much less expensive one but with a line that matched. I have often wondered about that magazine writer's knowledge and if he held stock in that certain rod company. I am sure that he was not considering the individual. His advice was suitable to him but certainly not to me.

The **ONE-PIECE ROD.** This type of rod has to be assembled with a tubular fiber glass blank. Split bamboo blanks of this type are not available. A one-piece rod should certainly be considered if it can be safely transported to and from the fishing grounds. Its action is considered a little smoother than a ferruled rod, especially one with a metal ferrule. A metal ferrule is to be avoided whenever possible, because it will wear with time to a loose fit.

The **TWO-PIECE ROD.** This type comes as a factory rod of tubular fiber glass with glass or metal ferrules or of split bamboo with metal ferrules. Split bamboo blanks and fiber glass blanks are available for assembling into rods. It would be nice if the glass blanks came with glass ferrules, but they are not available at the present time, at least not in the lengths required. If split bamboo rods or blanks are used, only those of the highest quality should be bought.

I have three expensive split bamboo rods, but I seldom put them to use. Fly rods, in most of this fishing, take a beating, especially when fishing from a boat, so fiber glass rods may be more practical for the purpose. The same care given a good split bamboo is needed for a fiber glass rod. Metal boat railings, power windows, and car doors are murderous.

About 10 years ago, I had my first experience with tubular fiber glass blanks. I relate this for any informative value. One of my many friendly tackle dealers recommended an 8-foot Lamiglas blank for use with a No. 9 line. He sent along the information on guide spacing and the how-to of judging the correct size to use for the guides. Frankly, I was very disappointed upon receiving the blank, since it looked like a piece of junk. After I assembled it, it still looked like junk. But after fishing with it for several days, I realized I had a masterpiece. The completed rod—with a cork reel seat and reel bands—weighed only 3¼ ounces and was used with success on 5 month-long trips to Mexico's salt water. I could fish this little rod for hours without tiring, and it was rod enough for the fish I encountered. I have not tried it for shad fishing, but next shad season I will be a little older and maybe a little weaker, so it will be put to the test. Over a day's fishing the average length of my casts may compare favorably with those made with the more tiresome outfit—heavier and longer rod and heavier line.

A few years ago, I tested a one-piece rod assembled with a Fenwick-Grizzly No. FF 1083 tubular fiber glass blank. It is 9

feet long and is matched with a No. 10 (280-grain) head. I was
so pleased with this rod that I made up a matched set—one with
a floating head and one with a sinking head. As I fish close to
my van, changing rods seems easier and faster than changing
lines, especially since I am the nervous type when fish are
around. I forget to properly string up the rod, and if you ever
fish with one missed guide, you will know what I mean. This
matched set is also ideal when boat-fishing.

The fly man is not always a one-rod man. He accumulates
several rods over the years—maybe seeking his dream rod. I am
acquainted with one fishing nut who went overboard. When he
took inventory, he found 16 rods in his garage. (At least it was a
garage until he bought so much tackle that there was no room
for a car.) He had 3 2-piece, high-grade split bamboo rods, 5
one-piece rods assembled with tubular fiber glass blanks, 4 2-
piece Fenwick Feralites, one No. 9 and one No. 10 2-piece
Scientific Anglers, Inc. rods, and 2 2-piece metal ferruled rods
assembled with Herters No. RB610 blanks—all salt-water-type
fly rods. That man has so many rods that it must add to his normal state of confusion.

The most popular rod length for this fishing is 9 feet. This
statement is backed up by years of observation. It is also backed
up by a check of fishing tackle catalogs. The one-piece fiber glass
blanks for this fishing are usually 9 feet long, with a maximum
of 9 feet, 6 inches. If we consider rod length only a 9-footer
should suffice for anglers of all ages.

It can also be stated that a No. 10 (280–300 grain) Shooting
Head is the most popular line weight and line type for salt-
water fishing. This statement could be argumentative, however.
But what tackle isn't?

I feel that any fly rod should be fished with for several days
before being approved of or disapproved of. I am thinking of one
fly man who after watching me cast wanted to try my rod. He
cast like an expert—the best casting I ever saw him do. He was

very surprised when I gave him the descriptive number of the blank. He had assembled one with a similar blank but sold it because he did not like it. The blanks must have been almost identical. Maybe he did not fish with it enough to get used to it.

CHAPTER 4

The Assembling of a Fly Rod

A fishing rod (please, not a fishing pole) is assembled with a blank and rod supplies (fittings). This is an interesting and rewarding pastime. With the use of a suitable blank and fittings, the resulting rod can be an excellent one. It can be built to an individual's specifications, and there is a personal satisfaction involved. There is also a saving of money—hard-earned or otherwise.

The **ONE-PIECE FLY ROD.** The blank will be of tubular fiber glass. And as completed rods of this type are not usually found in tackle shops and never—to my knowledge—in rod catalogs, it is a do-it-yourself operation. Because of its length—9 feet or more—it poses a delivery problem. A tackle shop could deliver a blank if a private parcel service such as the United Parcel Service is available. It will not be accepted by a U.S. post office. Sending one by freight is not to be considered. The best way to obtain a suitable blank is to find a local tackle dealer with a large supply. Sight down a number of them and choose one that looks straight (horizontally). Disregard vertical deflection (sag). All blanks have a certain amount of sag. Be sure it is a fly rod-type blank. I reject the ones that are crooked—like a pig's tail. Other methods are used by the experts in selecting a blank. The production manager of a well-known rod company and a former world's distance champion tests a blank by waving it, horizontally, back and forth. I could do that until my arms wore out and not come up with an answer. Another fly man selects a blank by placing the tip end on the floor and holding his left hand some 3 feet up the butt end while slowly rotating the blank with his right hand. He checked 2 of my seemingly identical blanks and found an uneven spot in one of them. I would reject all blanks found leaning against a wall in a hot storeroom, since they could acquire a "set" under such a condition.

The **TWO-PIECE FLY ROD.** The blanks are of metal-ferruled fiber glass or bamboo. Both are made up in a similar manner. Fenwick's rod blank catalog shows a number of suitable fiber glass blanks. Its No. FF 1085 (old No. 337) should be mentioned. The action is excellent for throwing the heavy flies used for this fishing. It has a pool-cue type butt, and if a metal reel seat is used, it will be necessary to use a dowel, since the standard seat will not go over this large-diameter butt. Since the butt section should not be longer than the tip section, it will be necessary to cut back the butt end. The dowel should enter the butt end for about 2½ inches and be cemented in place. The total dowel length is about 5½ inches. If a permanent butt is desired, allow for it. Either fiber glass or wood can be used; the former is preferred.

Herters catalog lists a 9-foot, 2-piece fiber glass blank that makes up into an inexpensive rod of good quality. The resulting rod is a powerhouse and is suitable only for the man of mighty muscle.

Let's go out to my nonprofessional tackle shop—a garage with no room for a car. I will show you how simple it is to build a salt-water fly rod—a popular one. As I make progress, the details will be given. The rod will look a lot better than the tackle shop, which seems to have been hit by a fair-size hurricane.

Here is a fiber glass blank that has been used by numerous fly men. It is a Grizzly-Fenwick No. FF 1083 (old No. 335), with an over-all length of 9 feet, 1 inch. With about an inch trimmed from the tip, a No. 6 top will fit snugly (it is not cemented in place at this time), using the cut-and-try method. It is fitted at this time to determine the over-all rod length.

Now to locate the position of the reel seat. Usually about an inch of space is left between the butt end of the blank and the end of the reel seat, resulting (in this case) in a finished rod of a maximum length of about 9 feet, 1 inch. But if you are going to be demanding, I can trim about an inch from the blank to make the finished rod exactly 9 feet long. The metal reel seat we are using is 3⅞ inches over-all, so the first ring of the grip is positioned 2⅞ inches from the end of the blank.

The **CORK GRIP.** The cork rings used on this job have an inside diameter (hole) the correct size for a perfect fit (tight) to the blank (at this grip position), and the blank has little, if any, taper here. I feel that the effort of finding corks with the right size holes is worthwhile in assembling any and all rods. Cork rings of this type are larger in outside diameter than the standard 1⅛-inch rings, which in most cases have holes so small that they have to be carefully reamed out to fit—a time-consuming effort. And the larger cork rings are more suitable, especially for the large-handed set.

The number of corks needed—they are a half-inch wide—is a personal preference. With medium-size hands, I am strictly a "12-cork man." With the first cork slipped over the tip and cemented in place, the balance of the needed corks are firmly pressed into place, cementing each cork to the blank and to each other, removing any excess cement with a damp rag. The rings should fit so tightly that no "cork vise" is required. However, a vise will be detailed later on. Be sure that the last cork fits so tightly that no grip check is needed. The standard grip check is a decoration only; it does not protect the edges of the cork, as advertised. It does not have sufficient outside diameter to do so. And decorations on a fly rod be hanged. It seems logical to buy the best rings available—rings that show few pits, although pits may show up while shaping the grip. The cork at the thumb position (on the top of the grip) especially takes a beating, since there is considerable thumb pressure during casting-fishing sessions.

The **METAL REEL SEAT.** A metal reel seat (the type of seat standard on factory rods) will be used to speed up the work. A cork seat requires much more time. Because the inside diameter of the seat is (in this case) about $\frac{4}{64}$ inch larger than the outside diameter of the blank, a filler is needed. The filler can be of wood, cork, masking tape, cardboard, etc. Just something to form a tight fit and—with a little cement—a permanent one. The seat must also line up with the blank. A piece of cardboard of the proper thickness for one complete circle of the blank is usually found available for this work, which also results in a good line-up between the seat and the blank. The cardboard (if used) is cemented to the blank—either in one piece or as 2 rings held in place with a few turns of twine and allowed to dry.

If I am working by myself (and am not being the big-shot instructor) and I reach this point in the construction, I look at my watch. If it is running and the hands point to near bedtime, I lay the work aside to dry; if it is siesta time (Mexican style), I take a nap; but if it is midmorning, I have no good excuse to stop working, so I proceed.

The next phase—an important one (although I read one article on rod building that did not even mention it) is to locate the guide "side" of the blank. I rotate the blank until it looks straight (horizontally) and mark the position of the guides on the down side—the side that has the most sag—using a circle of adhesive tape and an ink mark. Using the guide side (assuming that a circle has sides) I have suggested will give more power to the rod on the forward cast and less power on the pickup. Placing the guides on the opposite side will reverse this action. Rod companies seem to differ on which "power" is most important, but most of the amateur rod makers place the guides on the down side.

GUIDES. Snake guides are standard on almost all fly rods. The guides I use are of stainless steel, and being corrosion-proof, they are mandatory for a rod in salt-water use. They do wear after prolonged use of monofilament shooting line and have to be replaced from time to time. The hard chrome-plated ones found on high-grade factory rods wear much better, and recently became available to the public. Numerous fly-fishing experts like the foul-proof guides made by Aetna Products and Manufacturing Company, claiming they get more distance with them. The company furnishes a chart to suggest proper sizes and spacing. Some experts home-make similar type guides, also with rustproof wire. Personal preference rides again.

On this FF 1083 blank, we will use stainless steel guides of the sizes and spacing noted: One No. 1/0, 4⅝ inches down from the top, 4 No. 2/os spaced, 5, 7¼, 7½, and 8 inches, respectively; and 4 No. 3/os spaced 8⅜, 8¾, 9½, and 10¼ inches respectively. The stripping guide is a No. 8 carboloy guide and is located about 30 inches above the butt end of the rod, the distance depending somewhat on the length of one's arm and one's casting technique.

The snake guides are taken up one-by-one, and their ends are tapered down with a file or stone to allow the winding thread to wind smoothly up them for a perfect job. The guides are positioned both for spacing and "line-up" and are held in place with ⅛-inch strips of masking tape, placed far enough away from the ends of the guides so that the tape does not interfere with enough winding to hold them in place. The tape is then removed and the winding is completed. A short loop of thread is used before the last 5 turns are made so that the end of the thread can be put through the loop and the thread pulled under the winding. It is then trimmed close with a razor blade. There are several ways to control the thread during the winding process. After a few turns are made to secure the end of the thread, the spool can be held stationary between the knees. A rod winder can be bought or homemade, or a bobbin can be used. The bobbin is held between the knees and has the added advantage that the thread is held in tension and released as needed. (I have done so much rod winding that I feel wound up most of the time!)

Winding thread comes in all colors of the rainbow, including the color rainbow. For the least eyestrain a color that contrasts with the color of the blank is used. Light colors can be coated with preservative, which can be omitted on dark colors. Black thread has been used on many fine rods—it remains black with the use of lacquer or varnish. However, the color of the winding is not too important. Nylon thread in the sizes marked "A," "oo," "2M," or "3M," does the job. Finer thread can be used but will result in more eyestrain and more work. My favorite color is brown, but only because a fishing companion gave me a spool—"A" size—so large that I have enough thread to wind rods here and in the hereafter. Be sure to coat the windings to completely cover the thread for protection against wear and tear.

With the windings completed and the top cemented in place (lacquer will do it), we are ready for the final work—the reel seat. The twine is removed from the filler (cardboard in this case), and the seat is checked for a fit—a snug fit. In cementing the seat in place, the cardboard may swell a little with application of some liquid cement, so use a small amount of cement and work fast. I was slightly embarrassed the first time I demonstrated this method. The seat went halfway on and then froze. I almost wrecked the rod trying to remove the seat for another go at it. It seems easier to line up the seat with a reel in place, especially when working rapidly. Allow the cement to dry.

The cork grip is now shaped to fit the hand with the thumb

placed on top of the grip. The fine-tooth part of a wood rasp will do the rough work and No. 100 garnet paper the finish work. Some shaping can be done during the casting-testing. (Avoid sanding the line during the operation.) This finished rod will cast well with a No. 10 line of 280 grains—or a little lighter.

The customary way to cast this outfit is with the thumb in a sanded-out indentation on top of the grip. The grips found on the shorter rods—trout types—are not suitable for the long rods. They are made upside down. They are made for the man or woman with little fingers where his long fingers should be, and vice versa. And while we are on this gripping subject, it should be mentioned that rod companies cannot shape their grips on an individual basis. In due respect to many fine rod companies, their grips are usually too small in diameter for large hands and often too long for any hands of the human type.

A PERMANENT FIGHTING BUTT. The rod we have just completed is a standard model—only the grip has been customized. A permanent fighting butt is preferred by a number of fly men. It will be discussed here, although until I tackle a fish that outweighs me I can live without this permanent fixture. The operation is a simple one. The metal reel seat is positioned far enough up the blank to allow space for corks to be slipped on—from the rear—and cemented in place. The number of corks needed depends, of course, on the length of fighting butt desired. The reel seat will have to be open at both ends, so use a hacksaw on the closed end. Usually a permanent fighting butt is made with 4 corks (2 inches long).

The SEPARATE FIGHTING BUTT. This I like, and when and if I hang a whopper of a tarpon, yellowtail, or steelhead, I will use one if I am lucky enough to have it with me. To make one for any tubular fiber glass rod calls first for the removal of the closed end of the reel seat. A piece of wood or glass dowel to fit snugly inside the blank is needed. The dowel should enter the blank about 2 inches, and the number of corks used will depend, again, on the length wanted. A piece of cord is needed so that the fighting butt can be attached to the person.

The **CORK CLAMP.** The use of a clamp on the cork rings for any of this work will insure a perfect glue job. One can be easily made with 2 small-diameter threaded rods (4 washers and nuts—wing nuts are good) and 2 pieces of thin board about 2 inches wide by 3½ inches long. Holes are drilled on the centerline of the long side. A ⅝-inch hole is drilled at the center of this centerline so the boards can be slipped over the blank. This size hole will fit almost all fly-rod blanks. The billiard-cue type takes a ⅞-inch hole. A hole for the threaded rods is drilled on each side of the large hole at the distance necessary to clear the outside diameter of the largest cork to be used. Plywood can be used, but a smoother and easier drilling job is done with, say, a piece of half-inch-thick soft pine. In use, the clamp is left in place until the cement is thoroughly dry. It will not interfere with any progress. The corks will certainly not go anywhere after the nuts are firmly tightened. The length of the threaded rods needed will depend upon the maximum length of the cork grip. That length will take care of all other cork work.

Some expert casters prefer to shorten the blank at the tip enough to allow for a size larger top than the blank calls for, claiming that removing more tip removes any tip action. As an example, the FF 1083 takes a No. 6 top, but a No. 7 would be used under this condition. But one great caster, a former champion, told me to use the No. 6 top with this blank. His word is good enough for me.

The **CORK REEL SEAT.** Although the locking metal reel seat is standard on factory rods used in this fishing and is considered absolutely necessary to hold the reel securely, I really go for a well-made cork seat. For one thing, it is ¾ ounce lighter, which offsets to some extent the extra weight of the large reels used. And if made properly, it will hold the reel securely—I trusted a $135 Fin-Nor on such a seat with complete confidence. It is necessary to firmly seat one reel foot under one band and then slide the other band over the other reel foot with a great deal of force. Once I learned the trick, I used cork reel seats on all my rods.

Six of the best corks obtainable are cemented to the blank, leaving a half-inch of the butt end clear for the later installation of one cork to keep the bands from falling off. If a permanent fighting butt is to be used, 2 inches of butt are left clear. When the cement is dry (overnight, if possible) the cork is carefully sanded down to make a very tight sliding fit with the reel bands. This work is done completely, before anything else, so the thickness of the finished cork can be better judged for an even thickness around the blank. Care must be taken to avoid sanding down to the fiber glass. The bands are cut from ⅞-inch aluminum tubing and are half an inch wide. The bands can be swaged out with a homemade tool, or they can be shaped (on the inside) to fit the reel feet. One band can be cemented in place for easy reel line-up, but usually both are left free.

If you find a one-piece blank with the just-right action you like but cannot find this action in a 2-piece blank or finished rod, you can ferrule the blank with either a metal ferrule or one of fiber glass. This work requires a certain degree of skill. The blank has to be cut at just the right place if a metal ferrule is to be used, to insure a perfect fit, but this is not so true of a fiber glass ferrule. Making a glass ferrule consists of using a scrap of fiber glass of the proper size to fit precisely into the small end of the butt section for about 1½ inches and to extend out about 1½ inches to take the tip section. It must fit inside the tip section tightly enough to hold (by friction) while casting. The piece of fiber glass is cemented to the inside of the butt section only. Needless to say, the glass ferrule is slipped in from the large end of the butt.

If you find a factory rod that in your opinion has a super action, buy it. Use it until new guides are needed, strip it down to the buff, and then reassemble to your heart's desire with the features you like. This is entirely practical. If you wish to remove the reel seat on a new rod, it can be easily done with a little heat (on the metal only) and a little pressure against the butt cap of the seat (do not use pliers). Do not expose the glass, itself, to heat. With the seat off, a new cork grip of the length and diameter you like can be installed, working from the butt end of the blank so no guides will have to be removed.

CHAPTER 5

The Fly Reel

A fly reel for salt-water fishing will have to be more than a line holder. Certain requirements must be met and certain features considered.

TYPES OF FLY REELS. There are two types of fly reels: the quiet type, as represented by the Pflueger Medalist, with a drag mechanism; and the loud type—the screamers—as represented by the reels made by Hardy Brothers of England, with a click mechanism. The type selected is simply a personal choice.

I am a quiet, retiring gentleman (someone said use the word "shy" for a laugh), and I could not enjoy catching fish with a reel that did not scream like a Banshee. On the other hand, I know a quiet-type fly man who uses a Fin-Nor that does not give out even with a whisper. The "screaming reel" man is often accused of trying to attract attention, but if he uses the same type of reel on lonely beaches, the accusation is hardly justified. I especially enjoy a noisy reel when shad fishing. A jerk on the line kicks up such a racket that nearby shad fishermen come out of their daydreams with a start and get back to business. Surprisingly, they often start catching fish like mad.

The No. 1498 Medalist is a quiet reel that can be considered a "best buy," although I would not touch the type with a 10-foot salesman. The reel gets few complaints. The screws have a tendency, so I am told, to come loose. This is taken care of by removing the screws, dipping the threaded part in black lacquer, and firmly replacing. On a large fish, such as a 20-pound steelhead in fast water, the drag is considered inconsistent (that is what the man said when he lost the fish). Some alibi. I did hear of a Medalist burning up on a huge tarpon, but how often does one hook a huge tarpon?

I began my education in England, so my loyalty to old school ties may have influenced me to become an "English reeler." As soon as I could afford one—a Hardy St. John—I did so. That was in the 1930s, and to this day my affection for these reels has not wavered.

REEL CAPACITY. A large reel that will hold approximately 200 yards of backing and the fly line is needed. The capacity of a reel is determined by spool width and spool diameter. The amount of backing capacity in turn depends on the diameter of the backing and the type and the diameter of the fly line to be used. Let's consider the popular No. 10 fly line and a reel with a spool $1^{3}/_{16}$ inch wide and $3^{1}/_{2}$ inches in diameter. According to the Scientific Anglers, Inc. chart (using a 30-yard No. 10 weight forward line) the reel will hold about 150 yards of 27-pound-class Dacron or about 225 yards of 20-pound-class Dacron. With a No. 10 Shooting Taper and 100 feet of 20-pound (.0185-inch)-class monofilament shooting line, the backing capacity increases to about 200 yards of 27-pound-class Dacron, or 280 yards of 20-pound-class Dacron.

Another way to fill the spool of the reel is to buy 20- or 27-pound-class backing in bulk and then to fill the spool to within $^{9}/_{16}$ inch of the rim for a No. 10 weight forward line and to within $^{7}/_{16}$ inch of the rim for a No. 10 Shooting Taper line with 100 feet of monofilament shooting line. If Air Cel shooting line is used, the $^{9}/_{16}$ inch spacing is required. Scientific Anglers, Inc. does not give the diameter of the monofilament shooting line (I may need new glasses), but it is probably the popular size of 20-pound class. There should be from ⅛ to ³⁄₁₆ inch clearance between the last coil of fly line and the spool rim.

With the reel filled with backing up to the rim clearance noted, check the fly line capacity by tying the leader end of the line to the backing and spooling it on. If the floating line and the sinking line are to be interchangeable on the reel, use the floating line for the test, since it takes up more space than the sinking line. If 75 feet or more (in the weight-forward type) can be put on the reel without overcrowding, cut the remainder of the line off. This, with a leader, will allow a cast of more than 80 feet, which is a good distance for this type of line. Use this method to measure the sinking line. You may be able to get almost all of the line on the reel because of its smaller diameter. You will reverse the line (end for end) after fitting, of course. Loops at the ends of these lines will facilitate line changing. A loop in the backing large enough to go over the reel will make a good, easy-to-change connection. Just put the large (backing) loop through the line loop and bring it over the reel. It may be advisable to use an extra spool for these long lines.

As noted, reel capacity is much greater with a Shooting Head and its 100 feet of monofilament shooting line. Filling the spool to near-maximum capacity with this type of line results in larger coils of fly line but, what is more important, it results in larger coils of monofilament, which makes for easier handling and less kinks.

A spool ¹³⁄₁₆ or ¹⁴⁄₁₆ inch in width and 3½ inches in diameter will give about the right amount of capacity for this saltwater fishing. In size, this is a 3⅞ reel (at least this is true of the reels made by Hardy Brothers). It is easy enough to check the dimensions of any reel that interests you. The dimensions given here are not absolute requirements. A slightly smaller reel size should be sufficient. How much backing is actually required is anyone's guess. In years of this fishing, only once did I worry about a shortage of backing. I got hung up to a large salmon, and conditions were such that I could not follow the fish by either wading or bank walking. I had 175 yards of backing on the reel at that time. But for some reason, my fish seldom make the long runs described in fishing articles.

ADJUSTABLE TENSION. The reel's ability to put pressure on a fighting fish is another must. It rates in importance with capacity. The pressure is supplied by either a drag device or a click device. Usually the drag can be adjusted to enough tension to take care of the fish, but the click device on many reels has to be set at maximum tension to do so. I would like to see the "screamers" made with their present maximum tension a little stronger. But once the tension is adjusted for the leader tippet and the fish, it should be left alone. I do not think that the tension should be adjusted with a fish on.

SPOOL-FRAME CLEARANCE. It is important to have little clearance between the spool and the frame of the fly reel. Not so much because of what will happen, but because of what can happen if the line ever gets caught between the spool and the frame. I lost a nice-size yellowtail once because it did happen.

CORROSION. The salt-water reel should be fitted with corrosion-proof components. Most of the drag-type reels give little trouble in this respect, but a click-type reel that has a steel spring (or springs) has to be given special care. Dunking such a reel in the briny is not done in the best circles. I learned this the hard way—I had to buy new springs. Scientific Anglers, Inc. reels are without springs, so they are very corrosion-proof.

DURABILITY. Fly reels are durable if used for their intended purpose. Trouble occurs when a fisherman drops his reel on a rock or similar object more durable than the reel. Using a reel for years of excellent service (a case of love at first sight) only to have it badly damaged by being butter-fingered can make a strong man weep bitter tears. It is even tougher on a weak man. So if you are going to drop your reel on a rock, pick a soft rock.

THE LINE GUIDE. The first salt-water-type reel I owned did not have a line guide. When I noticed that there was some wear on the crossbars, I had to learn to strip off line with a parallel-to-the-rod motion—toward the stripping guide. With that learned, I do not need or want a line guide. The ring line guide on the St. George reel is not satisfactory. A ring guide on a wide reel is even worse and causes very uneven spooling. The "U"-shaped line guides on the Hardy reels will wear in time unless the line is stripped off the reel in a careful manner. Scientific Anglers, Inc. has hard chrome guides on its reels. I have used one of its reels for a year of fishing with no apparent wear. The line guide on the Medalist is considered the best of all.

REEL WEIGHT. Lightweight reels are popular, but it is possible to live with a heavy one. The Fin-Nor No. 3 model is a heavy reel, and with backing and line it seems to weigh a ton. But after getting used to it, the weight is not too noticeable. You may have to disregard some extra weight in order to get the features you want, or think you want.

REEL WIDTH. A reel with a narrow spool—something from 3/4 to 1 inch wide—is preferred to a wide spool. For equal line capacity the narrow spool has a larger diameter, which results in a little faster retrieve, more even spooling and, if shooting line is used, larger coils of monofilament.

SLIP CLUTCH REELS. What I call a star drag type is liked by the fly man who is afraid his knuckles will get bruised. The handle remains stationary during a fish's run. I have the feeling that getting the knuckles cracked just once teaches a never-to-be-forgotten lesson. I used a reel of this type for just one day's fishing and then sold it. Such a reel—the Seamaster is one—is supposed to be the thing on the Florida Keys. So if you want a reel that will let you wind in like mad with the fish going out like mad, try one. If possible, try it before you buy it.

LEFT-HANDED REELS. Most reels are adjusted for right-hand winding. If the reel is to be used with the left hand, check to see if it can be self-adjusted. Some reels have this feature; other reels have to be specially ordered.

EXTRA SPOOLS. Extra spools, complete with backing line, fly line, and leader are carried by fly men. The leader should be carried separately, since it can cause trouble if it gets wound into the line. The extra spool is practical for the use of weight-forward lines, because they are difficult to change while fishing. Shooting Heads create no problem. However, when I read that any line is easy to change in midstream, I feel that someone needs a head shrinker. It would take an arm as long as the rod, at least, unless the rod was supported by the bottom of the river. I am waiting for the day when someone will demonstrate this feat of magic. The big advantage of the extra spool would be to carry extra backing for the day a fish runs you down to the arbor.

REEL CARE. After a day's fishing, a reel will appreciate a good soaking in hot fresh water and a little back scratching with a toothbrush. All foreign matter should be removed. The complaint that the perforations on a reel are bad because they allow sand and gravel to enter the works is hogwash. You are not supposed to use a reel as a shovel—do not even rest it on the bare ground during the stringing-up process. After the reel is clean and dry, a coating of grease, such as Vaseline, is in order, especially on the springs, if any.

CHAPTER 6

Leaders, Knots, and Loops

LEADERS. The word "leader" was first used by a storekeeper —an acquaintance of Izaak Walton—and was a marked-down bargain on a highly overpriced article to "sucker" customers into his store. Izaak applied the word to fly fishing—a leader to sucker fish, not customers, into his net, not store. Or so the story goes. And since no fly man has proved to be smarter than old Izaak, the name "leader" has stood the years.

When a fish sees what a fly man refers to as a leader, the fish sees it as an outline—as a diameter. The fisherman talks "pound test" when he should be concerned with diameter. If we agree that it takes a certain minimum-size leader tippet to cast a certain size (weight) fly, what has happened to "good ol' pound test"? And what does pound test actually mean? Any meaningful testing should be done with the fly tied to the leader and all knots tested, up to and including the leader-line connection.

Leaders for salt-water fishing can be described as plain or fancy—a level leader or a tapered one. The knotless tapered leader is liked by many fishermen. It has a heavy butt and a tippet end (in various sizes). This leader can be discarded when it has been so shortened that the small end is too large in diameter for the fly and the fish. However, a tippet can be tied on to make the leader almost like new. The ones I am familiar with, but do not use, are made of limp monofilament throughout. I am a "hard nylon, soft tippet" guy. The tapered leader—with knots—can be bought or can be homemade from leader kits (the words "nylon" and "monofilament" are interchangeable).

A rule of thumb for matching leaders, either factory-made or homemade, to line is to use a leader with a butt section approximately ⅔ the diameter of the fly line.

The Mason Tackle Company of Otisville, Michigan, has a salt-water tie kit at a delivered price of $3.95 that will tie into a barrelful of good leaders. The material is hard (stiff) nylon. Soft (limp) nylon material is needed for the tippets. The diameters are given on each coil. A description, with the company's pound-test rating, is given.

30 yards	5 pounds	.009 diameter
30 yards	6 pounds	.010 diameter
20 yards	7 pounds	.011 diameter
20 yards	8 pounds	.012 diameter
20 yards	9 pounds	.013 diameter
20 yards	12 pounds	.015 diameter
20 yards	14 pounds	.017 diameter
20 yards	18 pounds	.019 diameter
20 yards	20 pounds	.021 diameter
20 yards	26 pounds	.023 diameter
20 yards	28 pounds	.025 diameter
15 yards	32 pounds	.028 diameter

The pound test has little meaning; the leader is tied according to the diameters.

Buz's Tackle Shop of Visalia, California, has this material in 44-inch strands—in all necessary diameters. It is sold by the dozen strands in an envelope marked with the diameter. Pound test is ignored. Coils or strands—take your choice. I take the dozen strands, uncoil them, and put a piece of adhesive tape around one end and mark the diameter on it. If this taping is not done, the coiled strands have to be uncoiled each time a single strand is needed. There is little waste whether coils or strands are used. By renewing the tippets, one leader will last almost forever, maybe even longer. The leader is tied up with blood knots (barrel knots) and the loop at the butt end is tied with a perfection knot.

The standard specifications for the tapered leader are 60 percent butt, 20 percent taper, and 20 percent tippet. One can, of course, tie up a suitable leader with three equal lengths of, say, .019, .016, and .013 inch, and a 24-inch piece of limp tippet down to, say, .011 inch, depending on the size and the weight of the fly and the shyness of the fish. I believe in using as small a diameter as practical. I do not like to step down a leader from a heavy butt to a light tippet without tapering, although it is practiced by experts. In the heavy stuff it is practical to drop down by $\frac{3}{1000}$, but in the smaller material $\frac{1}{1000}$ is safer knotwise. The relationship between the fly and the tippet and the fish and the tippet will be considered later on, under the various species. Something about 9 feet long will do for leader length.

The Shock Tippet is used by fly men on large fish such as tarpon and snook. This is strictly hearsay on my part. I have not used a Shock Tippet in my fishing. It is not needed—not so far —on the fish we are concerned with. I mention the tippet only to show that I am a "know it all" type. Such a tippet could save the day, so to speak, on a very large fish. Such a fish could mouth a standard-size tippet to zero test. A 12-inch length of 80-to-100-pound test monofilament is used between the fly and the standard leader tippet. It is tied to the tippet with a nail knot. It gives the fish something heavy to chew on. The size of the regular tippet used would depend on the "class"—recordwise—of the competition. This is a specialized type of fishing and is not too common.

KNOTS. There are two requirements for a knot. It must be simple to tie and secure. I am not interested in a knot that requires time and a college degree in engineering. Recently, I read that the Turle knot is no good. That writer sure knows how to hurt a guy. After using the knot for 40 years with confidence, it

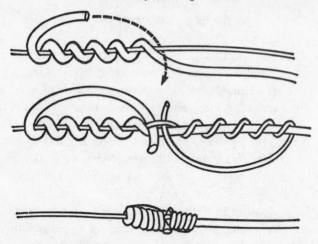

The blood knot (barrel knot). Start by holding the two strands, crossed at right angles, between the thumb and forefinger, with the ends sticking out about 3 inches. Wrap one end around the other strand several times. (We like 4 ½ turns on the finer stuff for extra safety, but in most cases 3 turns is enough.) Put this end through the fork formed by the two strands, shifting the knot to the other thumb and forefinger in the process so you can hold the twisted part and the end in position. Twist the other short end around the other strand, in the opposite direction, for the same number of turns, and poke it through the center of the lap. Pull up slowly and tight. The finished knot will look like the bottom view shown in the drawing. *From drawing and text courtesy of Scientific Anglers, Inc.*

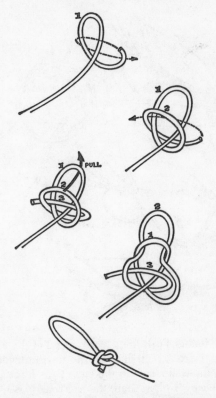

The perfection loop. Over the years, we've learned and forgotten how to tie the perfection loop perhaps 20 times. Bryce Dabler of Mason Tackle, which puts out an excellent leader-tying kit, showed us what we hope is going to be the answer to that problem. The answer is really all in the way that he describes the procedure of tying that knot. As Bryce puts it, you (1) make a loop *behind*, (2) *come around* in front, (3) *come around again in the middle*, and (4) pull the second loop through the first one. *From drawing and text courtesy of Scientific Anglers, Inc.*

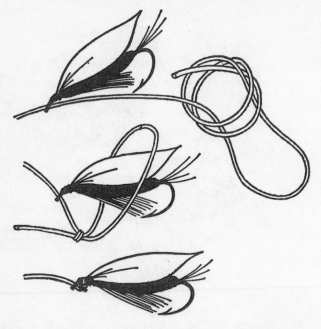

The improved double Turle knot. Put the end of the leader through
the eye from the front and slide the fly up the leader out of the
way. Make a simple slip knot in the end of the leader, bringing the
end around twice (rather than the customary one time, which
would make a single Turle). Put the end through these two turns,
pointed up the leader. Draw tight. Pull the loop snug around the
head of the fly, not on the eye or leader itself. *From drawing and
text courtesy of Scientific Anglers, Inc.*

1. Casting practice and instruction. (The barbs have been removed from the hooks.) *Courtesy of Fenwick/ Sevenstrand Co.*

2. Casting instructions. *Courtesy of Fenwick/Sevenstrand Co.*

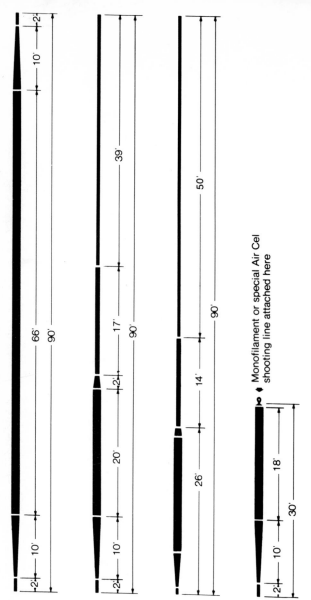

3. Line chart. a. A double-tapered line used for making a Shooting Head. b. A standard-weight forward-tapered line. c. A salt-water weight-forward tapered line used in bonefishing. d. A single-tapered line (Shooting Head). The single-tapered line is now made by Scientific Anglers, Inc., in the floating as well as in the sinking type. It is a better head than one made from a double taper, since the tapers are shorter. *Courtesy of Scientific Anglers, Inc.*

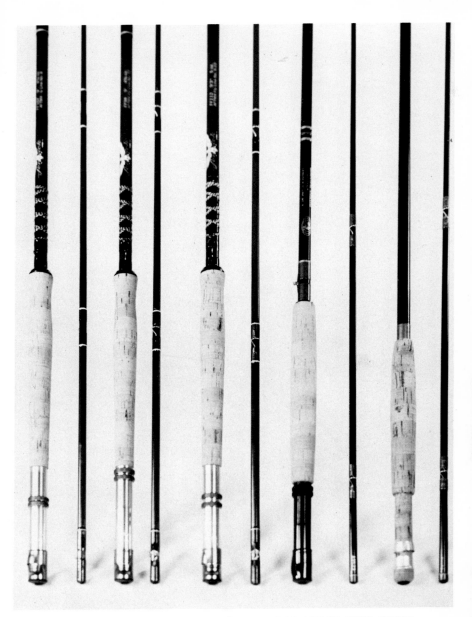

4. Factory rods. *From left to right:* Fenwick's FF107, FF98, FF112, Scientific Anglers, Inc. No. 9, No. 10. Note that the No. 10 has been remodeled with a cork reel seat. These rods are all great for this fishing. Fenwick's FF85 (not shown) is an 8½-footer that carries a No. 8 line, which is also used for salt water. The same can be said of Scientific Anglers, Inc., No. 8 rod.

5. The author with fly tackle. *Courtesy of Union-Tribune Publishing Co.*

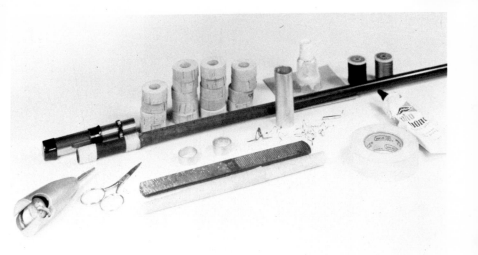

6. Materials and tools needed for rod assembling. The snake guides shown are now available double-chromed from Fenwick/Sevenstrand Company. These guides wear so much longer than the plain stainless-steel guides. Note at the bottom of the photograph the beveled sanding stick (dowel).

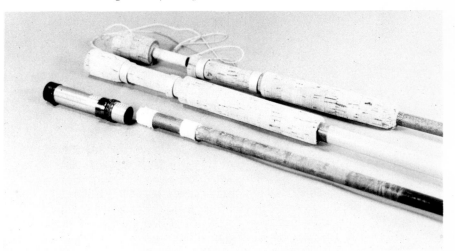

7. *Top to bottom:* a. Cork grip, Chuck Elgert cork reel seat and detachable (separate) "fighting butt." b. Cork grip, cork reel seat, and permanent butt. c. Blank with cardboard filler to take a metal reel #1 seat. NOTE: The cork reel seat is nothing new, but Chuck proved that it was perfectly satisfactory for salt-water fly rods. All my rods have this cork reel seat.

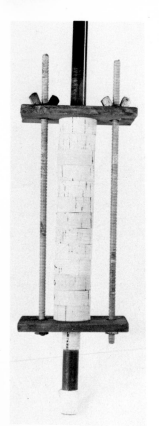
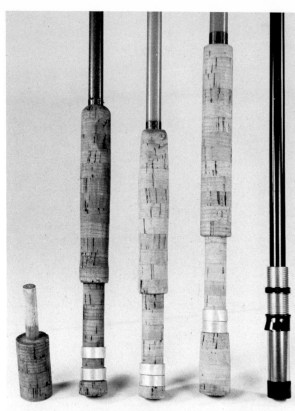

8. *Left:* Cork clamp. This easy-to-make cork clamp does a perfect job. Note the single wraps of cardboard for the filler for a metal reel seat.

9. *Right:* Fiber glass rod assembling. *From left to right:* An 8-foot, 3¼-ounce Lamiglas one-piece rod with a cork reel seat and a separate fighting butt; a 9-foot, one-piece rod with cork reel seat, assembled from an FF 335 (old number; new number, FL 108–10); a 9-foot, one-piece rod with cork reel seat and permanent 2-inch fighting butt, assembled from an FF 337 (old number; new number, FL 109–10); a 9-foot fiber glass blank with metal reel seat in place.

10. Guide winding. A snake guide, with its keepers beveled for easy winding, is shown taped in place. The large piece of tape shown in back of the guide is just to hold the thread end down until a few winds are made over the end and then removed. It is easier under actual construction to hold the end of thread against the rod blank with a thumb. (Tape was used for photographic work.) Five or 6 turns are made in front of the keeper end. When the wind nearly reaches the tape, the tape is removed and the wind is continued.

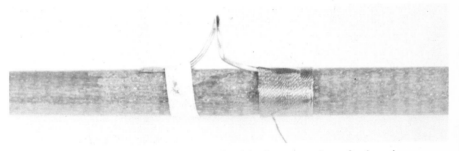

11. One keeper finished wrapped with the exception of trimming off the end of the thread. Do this carefully with a razor blade. The other keeper is, of course, finished in the same manner.

12. This shows the method of pulling the thread end under the wrap with a loop of thread.

13. Fly reels (all screamers). *Top row, left to right:* A 1929 Hardy St. John; a late-model Hardy St. John; a Hardy St. George with line guide. *Bottom row, left to right:* A Hardy St. Adrian with line guard; a Scientific Anglers, Inc., Model 10 with line guard (old rimmy); and a Scientific Anglers, Inc., Model 150.

14. Fly reels (all screamers). *Left to right:* A 1929 model Hardy St. John; a late-model Hardy St. John; a Hardy St. Adrian; a Scientific Anglers, Inc., Model 10; a Hardy St. George; and a Scientific Anglers, Inc., No. 150, with spool removed to show click mechanism—no steel springs to rust.

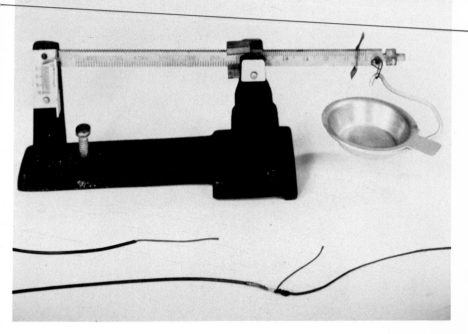

15. Line loops. Powder scales, line with coating removed, and finished loop with shooting line attached with standard Clinch knot.

16. Author wearing a Fish-n-Float and foot fins. Coffee pot shown is used as a refillable anchor. The award buttons on my fishing vest are supposed to prove that I am an expert. *Jeff Crowson*.

17. Author using a Fish-n-Float and foot fins in San Diego's Mission Bay. A bonito is netted. *Jeff Crowson.*

18. The well-equipped fly fisherman where wading is necessary (and it usually is). *Sam Nix*.

19. Materials and tools used in fly tying. The vise shown is nearly 45 years old and still going strong. Do not try to find one in a tackle store, since this vise is no longer made.

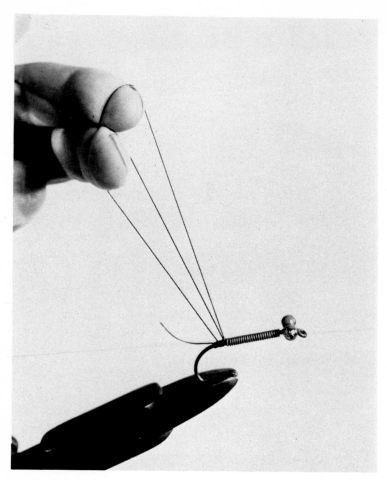

20. The half hitch. The hook is weighted with lead wire and large bug eyes. The hook shown is a No. 2, 3 extra-long, 1 extra-strong weighing $8\frac{1}{2}$ grains. The lead wire weighs $6\frac{1}{2}$ grains, and the large bug eye weighs 9 grains. Usually either the lead wire or the bug eye is used—not both. In either case, this is a lot of weight to cast, especially with material added that soaks up a lot of water.

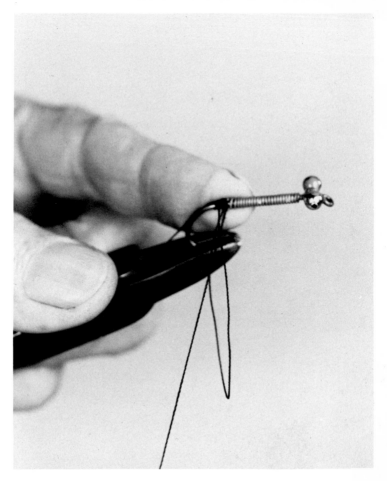

21. Completion of the half hitch. A finger is placed in position shown to hold the thread in place; the end of the thread is pulled through the loop with two fingers (see the previous photo), and pulled up tight. This is a lot faster done than said (or written). The photograph shows the finger of the left hand holding down the thread, but for a right-handed tier, the index finger of the right hand would be used.

22. Fly tiers. *Top row:* Twelve-year-old Chris Crowson, 12-year-old Chris Crowson, and George Stewart, Jr. *Second row:* Frank Lawrence, Hagen Sands, and author. *Third row:* Chris Crowson and author. *Fourth row:* Author and author. NOTE: To emphasize that a normal 12-year-old can do this tying. None of the above are professionals. These few patterns, fished with confidence, will outdo a hundred patterns and with a lot less confusion.

The improved Clinch knot. Some anglers prefer the improved Clinch knot for all flies; we think it is excellent for bass bugs and big flies, particularly those tied on ringed-eye hooks. Put the end of the leader through the eye from the front (from the top with ringed-eye hooks). Double it back up the leader about 4 inches. Twist the end around the leader 5 times, then bring the end back through the opening between the eye and the 2 twisted strands. Finally, put the end through the big loop inside the twisted part. Be sure to tighten this knot slowly, right against the eye of the hook. This is necessary to obtain maximum strength.

NOTE: The author feels that this knot is useful only for tying leaders to ringed-eye hooks. For attaching monofilament shooting line to the shooting head, use the standard Clinch knot. Do not put the end of the leader through the big loop inside the twisted part. *From drawing and text courtesy of Scientific Anglers, Inc.*

hurts me to learn that I have been using the wrong knot for attaching the fly to the leader—a fly with the preferred turned-
down eye—over the years. The reason I go for a hook with a
turned-down eye is because I like the Turle knot. It is illus-
trated just in case. . . .

For hooks with ringed eyes the improved clinch knot is used.
I use this knot because I do not know of a better one, but I don't
have to like it. Poppers are tied with hooks with ringed eyes because the turned-down eye is supposed to make it harder to lift
the popper off the water. That may or may not be true.

A nail knot is all the rage, but who needs it? Trying to tie this
knot with stiff monofilament seems a little complicated. But if I
used the knot I would leave about ¼ inch of untrimmed ends
and wrap them with winding thread and lacquer the thread to
form a smooth knot. It is suitable for the leader-line connection,
but it is not practical for the single taper-monofilament shooting
line attachment. A loop is much better. The shooting line weakens where it is attached to the fly line, and it must be retied from
time to time. Some of the boys at the casting pool use the un-
wrapped knot for the single taper-shooting line connection on
the basis that the connection is never pulled into the tip top and
guides, but that does not work out for most fishing. It is, of
course, possible to carry thread and laquer "streamside" to
smooth down the nail knot, but is the knot worth the trouble involved?

LOOPS FOR LINE AND LEADER. Loops can be used at
both ends of any type of fly line to good advantage. The loop at
the butt of the single taper line is necessary. Factory single tapers
are made with a loop (a separate piece of heavy squidding line
is spliced on the fly line) for the best possible connection to the
monofilament shooting line. I took apart one of the factory loops
and found that the coating of the line is not completely removed

but rather roughened up by slicing off some of the coating (finish). The wrapping is about ¾ inch in length.

A factory loop is, in my humble opinion, something to be removed and replaced with a self-loop. This loop is made by dipping the line end into acetone (being careful that the acetone does not work too far up the line) in order to remove the finish. A little light scraping is needed. The exposed core—about 1½ inches in length—is then doubled back on itself and wrapped and lacquered to form a loop barely large enough to take the shooting line. A short wrap of ⅜ inch will secure the loop. I think this loop is stronger than the factory loop with its ¾ inch of wrapping. It works better for ease of coming in or going out of the rod guides and tip top. All loops must be protected with lacquer or varnish at the first sign of wear. These loops must be straight, not curved, or the leader may twist up badly.

The leader can be connected to the line with a nail knot, a secure splice, or if a loop is used in the line, with a clinch knot or the standard leader loop. In theory, it would seem that splicing the leader to the line would be best. But the fly does not seem to go out by theory alone.

If you test the leader-to-fly knot, the leader knots and the line loops, do so by pulling on the line itself—with everything connected up as it would be under actual fishing conditions. I am not sure of the accuracy of my tests, but I found that the first knot to give way was the tippet-to-leader connection. The test was made with new material and newly tied knots. Knots do weaken in some cases with use and should be checked at intervals, depending on the amount of casting done. It is always good practice to retie the knot at the fly (or popper) after landing a fish—that is, if it bothers you to lose a fish or a fly. The line to the shooting line connection also weakens and should be retied from time to time.

CHAPTER 7

Wading and Floating Gear

The fly fisherman does almost all of his fishing in the water or on the water. If in the water, he needs some type of wading equipment that will keep him dry and, to some extent, warm. From my experience I can say that wading equipment is troublesome, expensive, or a little of both. Leaky waders is the story of not only my life but of the lives of many fly men.

STOCKING-FOOT WADERS. Stocking-foot waders were the type to first appear on the fishing scene. With a pair of wading shoes, the fly man had a fairly satisfactory outfit.

The old-timer dressed in wool socks, stocking-foot waders, wool socks, and wading shoes—in that order—for wading to within casting distance of his fish. At times, a little sand and gravel got into his shoes, but that was just something to live with. When he removed his wading gear, he had wet socks and waterlogged wading shoes to contend with. But since no one forced him into the water, he had only himself to blame. He thought he was having the time of his life . . . and he was.

When low-priced plastic waders were made available, the fly man, with a pair of carpet or felt-soled tennis shoes, was right in the swim. This was especially so if the plastics were only waist high. If his waders filled up with water from the top—and they did—he did one of two things: He stood on his head (preferably on shore) or he cut a drain hole in the waders at shoe-top level. You may ask why he did not remove his gear, pour the water out, and redress. Look at it from a practical standpoint. First, he has to find a little privacy, which is not always close at hand. He then has to strip to the buff and wring out his clothes, at times up to his collar button, put the wet clothes on, put his wading gear on and, if in the meantime he has not contracted pneumonia, go back to his fishing. Meanwhile back at the water, the fish have quit biting. But you do it your way and I will do it mine. These lightweight plastics are great when much walking is called for or when one is so "broke" that he cannot afford the real thing—that is, tailor-made boot-foot waders of the highest quality. In my case, at the present time all I have is a tailor-made dream.

WADING SHOES. Wading shoes can be the expensive ones made especially for the purpose, tennis shoes, or military combat boots—which are about 4 inches higher than the others. The extra height prevents some sand and gravel from washing into the boots, which at times so fills up the shoes that there is little room for the feet. The wader with a "B" foot and an "A" heel can usually get a better fit in wading shoes than in boot-foot waders.

Indoor-outdoor carpet or felt should be used on all wading shoes and for all wading unless the bottom is mud. Carpet is much lower priced than felt, which it seems to be replacing. But either carpet or felt will help the wader remain in an upright position, which in turn will help him do better casting. The carpet is available by the yard or as scrap pieces. Felt soles with the necessary cement are sold by tackle dealers.

A friend of my wife (but certainly no friend of mine) sold her on the carpet for the bathroom. This in one way was a "booboo." But I now have enough carpet to sole me from here to eternity. I can stand on the bathroom floor, mark the outlines around my wading shoes, use a razor blade, and remove two perfect soles of carpet. It will be time to retile the floor when it is more holes than carpet. So if you have trouble finding carpet, welcome to my bathroom.

After you have shaped the carpet, apply contact cement. The first coat will soak in but will form a base for the next application. In the meantime, remove any lugs from the wading shoes—this applies particularly to combat boots—in order to get as smooth a cementing surface as possible. When the first coat of cement is dry, again apply cement to the carpet and to the soles of the shoes and, when tacky, press in place. Wrapping twine or masking tape around the work will result in a better contact.

BOOT-FOOT WADERS. These waders are made in the chest-high type needed for deep wading. They are popular because they are sand-and-gravel-free and there are no wet socks and waterlogged shoes to plague the fisherman. They have two disadvantages, however: They are tiring to walk in, and the good ones—the only kind to buy—are expensive. The made-in-Japan waders are low priced but have not proved altogether satisfactory. The rubber is lacking in quality. Waders can be ordered with felt soles or can be soled with carpet.

The standard (stock) waders will not fit everyone. A man who is built on the slim side with corresponding feet is in trouble. The waders are too large in the waist and too wide in the feet. But they have to be long enough in the feet regardless of how they fit otherwise. On one trip I tried to get by with one size smaller than I usually wear (I was sent the wrong size), but after three days my toenails started going and finally were gone. And I mean completely gone.

WARM-WATER WADING. This is done with long trousers or walking shorts and carpet-soled wading shoes. The long trousers drag in the water but are good protection from the sun that hangs around this type of wading. Sand and gravel, as noted, are problems as usual, so if the weather is not blazing hot, I wear boot-foot waders.

Nothing need be said of hip boots. There are few uses for them. Their only use would be, say, on tidal bays that are mostly sand bars where knee-deep wading is done. I would not call them an essential piece of wading equipment.

WADING TECHNIQUES. If wading is a new experience, you should approach it with respectful caution—that is, if you expect to live a long life of fly fishing (or any other kind). The ability to wade is essential. It is not easy to learn to wade by reading about it. Practice in easy steps is needed. When ready to move in running water, upstream or down, move with legs parallel to the current. If there is no current, walk any way you wish—pigeon-toed, if you like. The first time I went wading, I wore hip boots and I almost shortened a long and happy fishing life by getting into fast water before I had the needed experience.

A life vest can be worn, and a wading staff can be used. A wading staff is used by numerous fly rodders, especially where the wading water is so unclear that the bottom is invisible or where the fishing water is new to the fly man. A staff is handy to pry the man back to shore and safety.

I have no use for wading staffs, for I am a daring young man. But they are used. They are made of various pieces of junk with a rope for making them fast to the person. A shovel handle, the old bait casting rod, a piece of tubing—name it a wading staff and it is. You can buy a combination wading staff and spare rod case if you have that kind of money. It is not advisable to carry a wading staff, a landing net, a creel, a fish stringer, and a spare rod into fast-flowing water at the same time unless you can swim tied up like a fish in a net.

FISH-n-FLOATS.* Last year a friend took me on a large-mouth bass bugging expedition. He supplied me with a canvas-covered inner tube with holes for my legs and a seat for my sitter. The device opens up a new fishing world. It is easy to transport by any means, it floats the fisherman over the deep holes (many of which are not visible), it is a quiet way to approach fish, it will float a man far enough out from almost any shore so he has a clear back cast, and it is, of course, less costly than any boat. This floating device can be deflated for easy storage, but since it is not much of a storage problem, I keep mine inflated and ready to roll. A factory job costs about $15.00 and is well worth it. The inner tube is not included in the price. The float comes in two sizes: regular for the man weighing up to 180 pounds and large for heavier men. The inner tube must also fit the man weightwise. There is a zipper for enclosing the inner tube, a zippered pocket for fly boxes, etc., and a shoulder strap to keep the device up while wading. Once you are afloat, the strap can be slipped off the shoulder for easier casting. The strap should be replaced when wading to shore or the device will drop down, trip the fly man, and lay him out on a muddy shore. A Fish-n-Float is not too practical for use during windy conditions. A small anchor can be carried, however, to keep from getting blown across the bay.

FOOT FINS. Fins are used with the floater and are strapped to the ankles. They have 5- by 6-inch blades that fold back with forward motion and act as oars when the legs are kicked backward. They are made in two sizes. The small size is advertised as large enough for Size 12 tennis shoes but fit only up to Size 10. The price is about $10.00. I cannot say how durable they are—I have not used them for a long enough time. Chest-high waders are needed unless the fishing water is warm.

* Tucker Duck and Rubber Company, Fort Smith, Arkansas 72901.

CHAPTER 8

Fly-Tying Instructions

All the successful fly fishermen I know tie their flies on hooks. Tying salt-water flies is easy once the hook is in the vise, but selecting that hook is difficult. Hooks are made under so many specifications that the hook subject is a very confusing one. Strangely enough, the importance of the hook is ignored by many, many fly men.

If I suggest you tie a fly on a certain size hook, without further descriptive information, I will be showing a lack of hook knowledge and I will be suggesting the size of the hook's gap (bite) and nothing else. Let's consider, for example, a No. 4 hook. It has a gap of ⅜ inch. This size hook is manufactured in a 5 extra-short shank with an over-all length of ⅝ inch. It is also manufactured in a 6 extra-long shank with an over-all length of 1¾ inches. And there are about 9 shank lengths in between. So describing a hook by size only is meaningless. However, you have not heard anything yet. And before you try to tie up a yellow belly sapsucker fly, you should hear more.

HOOK SPECIFICATIONS. We will take up the specifications in the same order that they are given in hook catalogs: (1) The eye of a hook is turned up, turned down, or ringed. The eye is also tapered, regular, or heavy (ball eye). (2) The shank length ranges from 5 extra-short to 6 extra-long, as has been noted. (3) In wire sizes, the range is from 1 extra-light (fine wire) to 5 extra-strong. (4) The wire is of steel of various carbon contents or stainless steel. (5) The finish on the wire is bronze, double bronze, tin, tin over cadmium plate, nickel, japanned, or stainless. (6) Hooks are made with various types of bends, points, and barbs. (7) It follows that hooks vary greatly in weight—a factor to be given considerable importance, since it relates to distance casting.

From time to time, I receive sample hooks that are not marked according to size, hook number, or description. This really bugs me! I am a little old for guessing games. No one will sell me a hook I really go for—it is not on the market. It would have the following specifications: a small turned-down eye—3 extra-long shank; 1 extra-strong wire; hollow point; perfect bend; straight; not offset bend, and of *stainless steel* wire. All-cock's S 218 comes close, but it is not stainless steel wire. Its bronze finish will rust through which, in turn, turns a lily-white fly into a brown one. The fly tied on this hook can, however, be used for a day's fishing and then discarded. A good soaking in fresh water at the end of a fishing day may help somewhat. The hook itself will tarnish if left exposed to a salty atmosphere.

A fly tying hook should be further considered for hooking quality, length of shank (which determines body length), the type of eye (for your favorite knot), the wire strength (as it relates to the fish), the type of point (for ease of penetration and removal), wire finish (resistance to corrosion), and type of bend. A straight (not kirby) bend is suggested.

Hooks are sold by the dozen, the half box, or the full box (100 hooks). You order a hook by size, the maker's name, and the maker's number. You can, if you wish, drive a tackle sales-man to the brink by ordering by specifications—a long list of specifications. Can you imagine a salesman going through every box of hooks in the store, searching for the hook that fulfills all your specifications? Fortunately (to lighten the fly tier's bur-den), some fly hooks are considered standard for some of our fish. These hooks will be noted by size, maker's name, and num-ber at fly-tying time.

Fly tying requires a few tools. A vise of some kind is essential, and vises are made with the tier in mind. The pedestal-type mount with a heavy base can be used, but the clamp mount type is preferred by most tiers. In use, the height of the vise is important. I tie flies with the top of the vise about 14 inches below eye level. These vises can be found in a price range of from less than one dollar to a bunch of dollars—like 12. A pair of sharp scissors, a spool of nylon thread (Size "A"), and a bottle of "goop" (such as fast-drying lacquer) will complete the minimum tool kit needed. A bottle of clear nail polish—with its small brush—is ideal for the cement work. The bottle can be mounted on heavy cardboard to keep it upright. A small can of lacquer and a can of thinner will take care of refills. Hackle pliers may be found useful on the small feathers. The fly materials needed will be discussed as we tie the various flies. The amateur tier has one advantage over the professional: The amateur ties his flies to please the fish. Remember, in fly tying, beauty is more than skin deep.

The **STEELHEAD FLY.** My first experience with salt-water-type flies began when I bought 3 steelhead flies in 3 popular patterns—popular at that time—and hooks and material needed for tying them. I was fortunate because my tackle salesman knew something about the then little-known game of steelhead fishing. After two days of driving, I arrived at the fishing grounds. After making camp, I sorted out my tackle, only to find I had lost two fly patterns along the way. I found the Royal Coachman, which I immediately tore apart to learn how to tie. I tied this pattern on the Nos. 2, 4, and 6 hooks I had bought. When I started to fish with these flies, I found steelhead. They were just waiting for my fancy offering. After some experimenting, I found the No. 6 size suitable to the fish and my casting ability. That fly, in that size, has been my lone weapon for 14 seasons of stalking this great fish.

The Royal Coachman is not the easiest pattern to tie, but once it is mastered, tying the other salt-water flies will be a breeze. Allcock's No. S 216 is a popular hook for steelhead flies and in sizes from 2 to 8s. It has a turned-down ball eye, 1 extra-long shank, 2 extra-stout wire, a hollow point, and a bronze finish. If we are going to be technical, we get a Size 5 fly when we use a Size 6 hook with its 1 extra-long shank.

The **ROYAL COACHMAN FLY.** With a Size 6 (in the S 216 hook) firmly seated in the vise (with the point concealed), we are now ready to tie a fly that may turn out to be too beautiful to use on a slimy old fish.

One end of a 2-foot length of nylon thread is secured at the eye of the hook by wrapping over it. Wind the thread tightly and closely back to the bend of the hook and tie off with a half hitch knot. The knot is formed as follows: Hold the first 2 fingers of the left hand (we are considering the right-handed tier) about 3 inches from the hook. Loop the thread over the fingers and then over the hook. Bring the thread back, clamping it between the fingers so it can be pulled through the loop. During the operation, the forefinger of the right hand holds the thread (at the hook) in place. Brush a little lacquer on the threaded hook to form a good base for the tying.

Tie in (at the bend of the hook) half a dozen fibers from a brown hen hackle. The fibers should be about ½ inch long. Half hitch. At the same location, tie in 3 or 4 strands of peacock herl. Half hitch. Wind the thread around the strands a few turns (for reinforcing) and wind thread and herl to form a tight ball. Half hitch. Tie in a short piece of red silk floss. Half hitch. Run the thread toward the eye of the hook for a distance of about ³⁄₁₆ inch. The floss is then wrapped to this point. Half hitch. Tie in another similar bunch of herl to form another tight ball. Tie in a large brown hen hackle (½-inch fibers) by the tip, half hitch, and wrap the feather around the hook 3 or 4 turns, and half hitch. Trim off surplus material as you go. If you have spaced the material carefully, there is room for tying in the white wing. If not, you can either commit hara-kiri or promise yourself better work in the future. The instructions, including the half-hitch knot, may sound complicated, but they are simple when carried out. It is easier done than said.

The white wing can be formed of impala hair, bucktail hair, fibers from a marabou plume, fibers from a large hen hackle, or segments from a goose quill. When using hair, a comb is used to remove any loose hairs—for an easier and better tie. The wing should be about as long as the hook. With the wing in place, a small, neat head is formed and coated with lacquer or varnish. Black thread will match the color of the herl closely enough. You now see before you a Royal Coachman fly in all its splendor. As far as I am concerned, this fly can be called a "Loyal Coachman." It has accounted for almost all of my steelhead.

It would help a little if you had an experienced tier at your elbow when tying your first fly, but he is not a necessity. With a little practice, your flies will gain that professional look, if that means anything. I get a certain satisfaction from catching fish on flies that I have tied. I use no others. You may feel the same way. Needless to say, the money that is saved is not to be sneered at.

There are at least 2 dozen patterns for steelhead flies. The fact that there are so many makes me wonder if the pattern or the method of fishing a fly is of the greater importance. The Royal Coachman, to the best of my knowledge, does not look like anything in the earth, on the earth, in the air, or in the water. But it works for me. I have complete confidence in it, and I know it will catch steelhead if they are around and if I fish it properly. All fly men do not use the pattern. But each has his own favorites.

The **SHAD FLY.** Several years ago, I spent half the night watching a professional fly tier mass-produce shad flies. His speed was unbelievable. The only cementing he did was at the head (finish) of the fly. He used a bobbin with the tension adjusted so the weight of the hanging-down bobbin took the place of half hitches. I do think that a little more cementing and some half hitches would have resulted in a more durable fly. A fished fly gets some wear and tear.

The Carl Ludemann pattern is the standard for shad, at least on the West Coast, where it is found in the fly box of almost all shad men. The tail is a few red hackle filaments, the body tight wound oval silver tinsel, the hackle of soft white hen hackle, and the head is a turn of red chenille. The tinsel should be touched up with cement for a more durable job. At times, a weighted fly is needed to get down to the fish. Lead wire of .025-inch diameter is tightly wound on the shank before any other tying is done. A few wraps of thread and a little cement (lacquer) will secure the wire. If the shank is not solidly wired, it is suggested that the weight be placed near the eye. This imparts an up-and-down nodding effect to the fish. The fish considers this a friendly gesture. But the fly man is conning the fish.

The Allcock S 217 is used for these flies. It is similar to the S 216 recommended for steelhead flies but is nickel-plated to give more flash to the fly. I will never know if the extra flash is used to please the fish or the fisherman. The S 216 may be just as good. Sizes used range from 2s to as small as 10s.

Since almost all shad are released, a hook that is easy to remove from the fish's mouth is popular with the fly man and—you may be sure—with the shad. A Jamison barbless (Herters No. 303)—a turned-down eye, 1 extra-long shank, 1 extra-fine wire hook—is suggested. A weighted fly is usually used. The shad does not find this type of hook easy to spit out, but it is easy to remove. In sizes smaller than 8 the point may be too close to the eye for good hooking. A size 4 is the largest stocked.

The **MARABOU STREAMER FLY.** The Hugh Turner pattern, in the standard or improved version, is a great fly, which has proved successful on almost all salt-water species. The standard pattern is tied as streamers usually are—with the wing tied in near the eye. The improved version has the wing material tied in as a tail, which seems to give the fly more action, and it also results in a maximum over-all length of fly when marabou filaments are used.

The pattern is easy to tie, but selecting a hook for streamers is even more difficult than for other flies. Herters No. 711SS is stainless steel wire, so it is a popular hook, but it has features that are undesirable. The specifications: a large-ringed eye, regular-length shank, 1 extra-strong wire, and improved Kirby bend (offset). The offset can be easily straightened while cold, but the eye has to be red hot for turning down. The large ringeye is not liked because of size or type, and the shank should be longer. The hook weight is 8½ grains.

International Hook Supply of Denver has a Mustad No. 79473 hook that has a turned-down eye, 3 extra-long shank, 3 extra-strong wire, and a tin-over-cadmium plate finish that is good for salt-water use. Its weight in Size 2 is 12 grains—certainly not a lightweight hook. It is almost rustproof.

The Eagle Claw No. 255SS in Size 2 would make a fine hook for flies tied with little, if any, body. It has a turned-down eye, appears to have a 3 extra-short shank, heavy wire, and O'Shaughnessy bend. This hook is popular with Irish fly men. The hook weighs 7½ grains.

If you are getting weary with the hook subject, let's tie one of these super marabous—the improved version. Just place a streamer-type hook—something in Size 2 with a 3 extra-long shank—in the vise and we will get with it. The operations are similar to those used before; only the materials are different. Take up a large (long filaments) white marabou plume and cut off as large a bunch of filaments as you can comfortably hold in the hand and tie it in at the bend of the hook. It takes a large amount of material, since it shrinks when wet. Tie in—also at the bend—a short piece of wide flat silver tinsel and a short piece of large white chenille (Size 9). Wind the thread up the shank to within $\frac{5}{16}$ inch of the eye, and half hitch. (I have not mentioned other half hitches needed, as you now know when to use them.) Wind the chenille to this half hitch, and half hitch. Spiral wind the tinsel to the same place, and half hitch. You now have before you the important part of the fly. From here on you can be on your own. Red chenille can be used to complete the fly, filaments of marabou can be tied in at the top and bottom, or a soft white hen hackle can be wound on. Make a neat head, lacquer it, and you have a fly second to none, with maybe one exception. The marabou and chenille used on this fly soak up water like sponges, and the fly gains considerable weight. Some tiers prefer to use bucktail hair. They claim bucktail hair makes a more durable fly. But marabou has its followers. The longest fly I can tie with the longest filaments (marabou) available, using a Size 2, 3 extra-long shank hook is about $3\frac{1}{2}$ inches.

There may be times when a longer fly, say 5 inches or more, is needed. To accomplish this, use not just the marabou filaments, but the tip portion of the complete plume. One expert uses flies up to 7 inches long on striped bass. This calls for well-combed bucktail hair that is tied in top and bottom, close to the hook eye. My expert friend does not consider a body of any kind necessary, and he should know.

The filaments of the marabou plume are so light in weight that they are difficult to handle in the slightest breeze. If you are right-handed, any breeze should come from your right side. One tier told me that he opened a one-ounce sack of plumes and they got away from him and went into orbit near the ceiling of his workshop. He said that if he wanted a special size or color, he would patiently wait for that particular plume to float within reach. This could have happened. Most fly men are completely truthful.

The **BONEFISH FLY.** The Hagen Sands Special bonefish fly does not look like anything I would go for if I were a bonefish. It must, however, be a good imitation of something in the shallow bonefish flats. It is a great favorite on the Florida Keys, although I would argue with the experts about the hook they use. I am looking at one of these flies, and the hook looms up like a lighthouse in the fog. All I can see is the hook. You would think that so visible a hook would chase Mr. Bone back to Africa. The hook is a size 1/0 with a standard shank and of very heavy wire, tinned. The fly pattern is on the slim side and not over 1½ inches long. To me, at least, the hook is much too large for the fly—a mismatched team. A Size 4 of similar specifications would seem more appropriate. However, one should not argue with experts on their home grounds.

Let's put a Size 4, Eagle Claw No. 255SS hook in the vise to see how we will come out. About a dozen white bucktail hairs about 1½ inches long are tied in on top of the hook close to the eye. This is for the body. One yellow hackle and one grizzly hackle is tied in (in that order) on each side of the hook to flare out. A neat black head completes the fly. I used this pattern and a pink marabou streamer pattern on the same size hook but in the No. S 216 for some successful fishing. With such a variety of aquatic life on the flats, the fish should be interested in any fly about 1½ inches long—if fished correctly.

The **SALMON FLY.** The fly used on the Pacific variety of salmon is tied on the Mustad No. 7970 Limerick hook. It is a turned-down eye—ball type, regular-length shank, and 5 extra-strong wire hook. The point is hollow ground but still coarse, so sharpen well. The pattern calls for an oval tinsel body—gold or silver—with a brown hackle heavily tied and a brown bucktail hair wing, tied in close to the eye and tied down at the bend of hook. It is a shrimp-type fly that should work on bonefish. The hook weighs 7.5 grains in Size 4. Size 6 is also popular.

The **SALT-WATER POPPER.** The hook used is Herters No. 993DH. A ringed eye—correct for poppers—with a 3 extra-long shank "S" humped, regular-weight wire, round bend, needle point, double-bronzed hook. This hook is the best I have found. The wire has proved strong enough, which might lead one to believe that regular-strength wire would be satisfactory for other hooks. The double-bronze finish will corrode, but until such a hook is made in stainless steel wire, the problem will have to be lived with.

To tie this popper, a Size 2 hook is placed in the vise and solidly wrapped with thread from the eye to the bend to provide a better bond with the cork. The cork in the shape of a cylinder, for this size hook should be ⅜ or ½ inch in diameter and 1 inch long. The length of the cork is determined by the length of the shank, less the length needed for tying on the tail. A slit is made in the cork with a fine hacksaw blade—the set can be taken out of the blade with a stone—just deep enough to fully take the hook. The fit of the hook to the slit must be a tight one. A generous amount of cement is forced into the slit and the hook pressed home. Glu-Bird is a good cement for this work. Plio-bond, contact cement, and epoxy are also used. White thread can be wound around the cork for a viselike effect, but this is not altogether necessary. However, it could be used as reinforcing. Several years ago I watched a professional tie bass bugs. He made a little groove around each end of the cork and then made enough turns of thread around the cork until the grooves were filled to the level of the cork. This was done solely to better secure the cork to the hook. When the cement is dry, the cork can be rounded at the rear, for beauty's sake only, painted white with a red head, and set aside to dry.

A tail of white marabou filaments is tied in at the rear of the cork (at the bend of the hook) to complete the popper. For this size popper the tail should be about 2 inches long. White bucktail hair can also be used for the tail material. A large, soft white hen hackle can be wound on at the same position for more popper action—factual or imaginary. I am not sure that it is necessary to paint the cork. At least it can do no harm. The disturbance made by the cork in the water and the wiggling tail should do the job. A popper drives a fish almost out of its mind—to say nothing about the fly man when the fish clobbers it.

A much larger popper is popular along the East Coast and in the Florida Keys. The hook used is a 1/0, ringed-eye, 3 extra-long "S" side-humped shank, 2 extra-strong wire with a nickel finish. The $\frac{5}{8}$-inch diameter by $1\frac{1}{2}$-inch corks come with a hole drilled lengthwise through the center of the hook. I tied some of these poppers but placed the hook in a slit at the bottom of the cork. A few were painted yellow with a red head, and yellow bucktail hair was used. The rest were painted white with a red head and had a white hair tail. They were 4 inches long. I did not find the large tarpon and snook, which were supposed to snap these poppers up with vigor. My experience with poppers of this size is limited. The 1/0 hook weighs 12 grains.

Matching the size of the popper to the fish takes a little doing, and the results can be surprising. I fished a month of daylight mornings testing various sizes on a bayful of bonito. The No. 993DH hook was used throughout in three sizes and with corks to match. Starting with Size 2 with a $\frac{1}{2}$-inch by 1-inch-long cork, the fish made passes but were not too interested. I then went down to Size 4 with a $\frac{3}{8}$-inch-diameter by $\frac{3}{4}$-inch-long cork. This size did not get much better results. But with a Size 6 hook with $\frac{1}{4}$-inch-diameter cork by $\frac{5}{8}$-inch-long cork, I was in business. This was the popper—the size—they had been waiting for. The fish were in the 2-pound class, but this baby popper did just as well on the larger offshore fish.

The over-all length of the little popper is less than 2 inches. And the ⁵⁄₁₆-inch gap is considered much too small for ocean fishing, but when the actual fishing for bonito is discussed, my story will sound like a typical fishing magazine article. I was proud of my brainchild, but when I sent one to the big boys of Scientific Anglers, Inc., a letter came back insinuating that I was suffering from the rattles. They described my pride and joy as fantastically ridiculous. They sure use big words back East.

Corks are sold in all shapes and sizes. The tier can buy corks the way he wants them, or he can do the shaping and cupping himself. The larger corks can be cupped for more action, but do not cup them to such a thin edge that they will chip off.

Balsa wood is used in popper construction. A simple-to-make jig is used to cut the slit for the hook—a slit perfectly centered and of the proper depth.

Two pieces of molding, say, $\frac{1}{4}$ inch by 1 inch, are mounted parallel on a workbench or a similar stationary board, spaced to take the square section of balsa wood selected for the work. A finish nail is centered in this space, sharpened to the width and height needed to form the slit for a tight fit with the hook to be used. The 3-foot length of balsa wood is fed through the jig with perfect results. The bottom corners are slightly rounded, and the top is rounded. Segments are cut off at a slight angle to give a slanting face to the popper and a sloping back. The hook is cemented in place, either before the finish sanding or after. The 3-foot lengths of balsa wood come in all size square sections needed for popper construction. A jig will be needed for each size of balsa wood.

CHAPTER 9

Fishing from Shore

Fishing from shore in this sense will include all fishing that is not done by boating. Wading a river has been discussed.

FISHING FROM JETTIES. The words, "is dangerous to your health" also applies to fishing from a rocky jetty. The fly man, especially, in his casting for distance, uses a follow-through that may result in a fall or even a ducking in the ocean. Shoes with carpet or felt soles are necessary. A casting platform in the form of a rock with a large, level surface is the goal.

The highest award I ever received was to find, one morning, that one of my young fishing companions had painted my name on my favorite rock. The large red letters could be seen for a mile. This rock—a great casting platform—was regarded from then on as my personal property. "Long live the King" refers to this "Michelangelo."

Depending on the individual, the casting is done at the water's edge or at various positions on the slope of the jetty. It is a matter of back-cast hazards, which depend somewhat on the condition of the tide. During the high tide, one can stand at the water's edge and clear the top of the bank with his fly, but at low tide the problem is much greater. Here one learns to use a very high back cast, or he casts from farther up the slope.

I fished a jetty with two experts—one a former world's distance champion. They did their casting some 20 feet from the water so they could avoid any back cast problem. Regardless of tide conditions, these experts could reach the productive water.

A small piece of netting at their feet prevented the retrieved line from catching in crevices and on rocks. The sight of them carrying the netting bothered one fish and game officer, since netting is illegal in that area. Casting from jetties is more difficult than it is at a casting pool, but the fishing is, usually, much better.

One of the problems on the back cast is people. One day I caught 10 bonito and one San Diego City gardener. Another time I suddenly changed direction in my casting and hooked one of my most favorite fishing companions. Actually, this is not a joking matter. It is very unfunny to the person getting hooked. If the barb of a hook gets buried in the skin, the services of a doctor are required. My record, over many years of fishing, is no under-the-skin hookups on any person but myself.

BEACH FISHING. Fishing from beaches is usually done by wading as far out as possible and casting from that position. In the open ocean, the bottom drops off sharply and the wading-out distance is very limited, but every bit helps the back-cast problem.

TIDAL BAYS. Wading in tidal bays creates no problems unless the bay is cut with channels. Four years ago, 4 local fishermen crossed a channel at low tide to fish a flat. When the tide came in, they were in trouble. Two men managed to get back to shore on their own, but the other 2 had to be rescued by the Coast Guard by helicopter. (A Fish-n-Float would be ideal under such conditions.) One afternoon, I saw several persons, including several kids, looking for shells on a tidal flat. They were strangers to the area. I warned them that if they did not get across the existing channel within the next hour, swimming would be the order of the day. In this certain locality, the tide comes in through holes in the rocks of the jetty; to most persons, the water looks like an inland lake, but the tides are, at times, seven-footers.

CHAPTER 10

Fishing from a Boat

There are two prime ingredients for a successful fly fishing trip on the ocean: a man who knows the ocean and can find fish, and a boat suitable for this space-consuming way of fishing. If one ingredient is missing, the trip will turn out to be just another boat ride.

THE MAN. The man at the wheel, usually the boat owner, has to know the signs to look for—diving birds, breezing fish, blue (not green) water—when hunting fish on a broad expanse of water. And he must have a keen interest in fly fishing. How he gained the knowledge is not important. How he fished before taking up fly fishing should not be held against him, at least not openly.

Casting ability—getting the fly way out there—is advantageous, but hardly a strict requirement. I have, for instance, caught feeding bonito with little more than a 9-foot leader out past the rod tip-top. And I'm not too certain fishing ability is a must, if the fish are in the right mood.

When a trip is contemplated, a wise move is to first check the previous day's fishing report given by the local sport-fishing fleet. Weather forecasts also should be checked. Fog, among other things, can bring the trip to a grinding halt.

My experience with this type of angling has been gained in the various kelp beds off the San Diego coast. Rarely, however, have both necessary ingredients been present. One of the men who asked me to be his guest for a day's fishing even forgot his fly rod. But he did take along a camera for the pictures that say, or are supposed to say, more than a thousand words.

THE BOAT. Most of my offshore fishing has been from an 18-foot outboard with an 8-foot beam—the maximum width for trailering. The boat is equipped with one large and one small motor, the latter for safety's sake. The controls are in the stern and do not interfere with casting. All gear, with the exception of the fishing tackle, is stored in two lockers located on either side of the boat. A canvas bait tank—with a cover to be used in rough water to prevent the bait from going back home—with a pump is used to keep a scoop of bait alive for chumming purposes. The benefits derived from chumming will be discussed later. A large hand net for the fish, a dip net for the bait, and 2 anchors complete the equipment. Two anchors are carried as insurance against losing one. Anchors have a bad habit of going overboard and not coming back. (One dark and stormy night, I was told to get out the anchor and drop it overboard. This might have done some good if I had been told to make the anchor rope fast to the boat.)

After launching the boat and picking up a scoop of bait at the bait barge, we head for the fishing grounds—timing our departure soon after the sport-fishing boats get under way. One of these boats at anchor with "fish on" is our goal. At that time, there will be a chum line running out for a considerable distance from the stern of the sport-fishing boat, and we are interested in that chum line. However, good sportsmanship—the regard for the rights of others—is shown by us. Plenty of room (water) is allowed between boats. The fact that the sport-fishing boats carry rifles to discourage seals has nothing to do with it. Once our anchor is down in a holding position, we get to our battle stations—one in the bow and one in the stern. This is on the assumption that there are only 2 men aboard. And regardless of what "handed" we are, there is no casting interference.

If both fly men are right-handed casters, the one in the stern casts to starboard and the one in the bow, to port (making his casts with an eye out for the stern caster): Two southpaws work the same way, but to opposite sides of the boat. A right-hander and a southpaw cast from the same side of the boat.

The actual fishing will be covered under each variety of fish. A matched set of outfitted fly rods is carried by each man, room permitting. One rod of the set is rigged with a sinking head and a streamer fly and one with a floating head and a popper. A streamer also can be used with the floating head.

Before you dash wildly out to buy a boat and get with this fishing, you should realize the expense and work involved in owning a boat. But it works out fine for professional men and gangsters (no insinuations intended) who do not have the time to run all over the country seeking the elusive fish. And if it were not for these men, I—a poor old fishing tramp—would not be able to enjoy this fishing. I have a warm feeling for these men although, so far, I have not been the guest of any bad guys.

CHUMMING. The small-boater chums for the same reason the sport-fishing boat does—to locate the fish by bringing them to the surface and keeping them within casting range. The amount of bait used by the sport-fishing boats may be as much as a scoop at a time, but the small-boater with a bait tank holding not more than 1½ scoops, tosses out bait in a very meager fashion—on a now-and-then basis. The results obtained are often surprising. On one trip, we kept the fish around the boat for 4 solid hours. What a day that was. Chumming does pay off.

The **ROTATION SYSTEM.** With more than 2 fly men aboard a boat of almost any size, a system is needed—with someone in command—so each man is assured of his turn at the fish. On a large boat, a charter boat type, there is so much super-structure, such as a cabin, mast, lines etc., that fly casting is limited to one man at the stern and one at the bow. And since the stern is the most productive position on a boat, it works out to one man casting at a time.

This rotation system does not reduce the individual's fish count. As soon as the first fly man (of the system) is hooked up to a fish, which—with so many fish around the boat—could be on his first cast, he moves away from the stern area to fight and eventually land his fish. This allows the next man to get into the act. If the system is conscientiously followed throughout the fish day, the net result will be more fish on board than by the custom-ary way—all the fly men rushing to the stern and casting, or rather trying to, at the same time. It turns into a mob scene with the fly men hooking each other, the skipper, his crew, and the superstructure. Such a display of flies would be better related to a tackle store. The roll cast was suggested by one man. Roll casting uses the whole side of the boat, so that is not the an-swer. Mob-type fly fishing does not result in any lifetime friend-ships.

CHAPTER 11

Fishing the West Coast (U.S.A.)

STEELHEAD. Like the salmon and the shad, steelhead live the greater part of their lives in the salt water. They ascend the free-flowing rivers of the West Coast on their spawning run. Many of the larger rivers have both a summer run of steelhead and a later migration of larger fish. There seems to be an overlapping of these runs, since the fish are present continually from late spring through the following winter. Fly fishermen usually concentrate on the summer run, when conditions are more favorable. Lower and clearer water puts more steelies "on the beach."

The Klamath River has a summer run of fish averaging 2 to 5 pounds. Last fall, one of my steelheading friends beached a good fish of 7 pounds, 4 ounces. The fish are supposed to run larger in the river below the influx of the Trinity River, but I have not found it so. I did land one 12-pounder, but it had been in the river for some time—long enough to take the brilliant coloring of a rainbow trout. The time to fish this mighty river is from mid-August in the lower river to December in the upper stretches. Steelhead have been fly-caught in December, but water and weather conditions are unpredictable at that time. The success of a fishing trip depends on pleasant weather and water conditions as well as available fish. Having the fly line freeze in the guides does not thrill me.

Oregon's famous Rogue River, some 25 miles below Grants Pass, has produced fish from 4 to 10 pounds. This water is some 90 miles upriver from the coast.

The big deal now in steelhead fishing is in British Columbia's

Kispiox. It is about 2800 miles from my home and not of my experience. But from reliable reports, it must be great. These fish often are winners in fishing contests and range from 10-pounders to well over 30 pounds. It is the place for fly men who can spend from September to snow time because there are days, sometimes several of them, when the water is not suitable for fishing.

Trout tackle just will not do for steelhead fishing. I have a garageful of suitable rods for this fishing. Sorry, the garage is locked up, but I will describe some suitable rods. A long rod is needed, with the 9-footer the most popular length. One made from a one-piece blank, Fenwicks in Nos. FF 98 and FF 112—a 9-footer and 9-foot, 3-inch rod, respectively—are well liked. Scientific Anglers, Inc. lists a 9- and a 10-system rod that is also gaining in popularity. The 9-system rod, but with the 10-system Shooting Taper (head), is used by the big boys on the Kispiox. A No. 10 Shooting Taper line will work on these rods, and your rod should be selected with this line weight in mind. The fly reel is the most important part of your outfit once the fish is on. The larger the steelhead, the more controversial the subject of reels becomes. The reel for the oversized fish of the Kispiox can be an $18.00 Medalist No. 1498 up to a $135.00 Fin-Nor or a $142.50 Bogdan. A hardy St. John was just right for my steelhead fishing.

The single taper line—a Shooting Head—with 100 feet of 20-pound (.0185-inch) limp monofilament shooting line backed by about 200 yards of 20-pound-class Dacron will be suitable for this fishing. A 9-foot leader tapering down to .010-inch tippet (or a size larger) will take care of steelhead up to 8 pounds, with a .0135-inch (12-pound-test) tippet used on the giants of the Kispiox. The clearness of the water has a bearing on tippet sizes as well as the weight of the fly.

There are at least 30 patterns of steelhead flies. Every steelhead river has its local hot-shots who come up with patterns. They prove deadly maybe because the fly is fished with confidence. Some flies that were hot years ago are no longer found in the steelheader's fly box. From my experience, I can only say that if I were going to any steelhead river, my fly box would be loaded with Royal Coachman flies in Sizes 2/o down to Size 6. I would tie the 2/o and 1/os with the goose wing favored by anglers on the Kispiox, and the others with hair wings. If all steelhead patterns were checked, a few, at least, would be similar to the Royal. The tier does run out of wanted materials at times. Maybe he did a little substituting. And maybe he had trouble with the herl at the bend of the fly unraveling. (He should have reinforced the herl with winding thread.)

Almost all the steelhead experts I know take their fish on a Royal Coachman. I know of only one expert who does not. His fly does not have anything in common with the Royal. But you can be sure he fishes his pet offering with full confidence. And I think that confidence is of utmost importance. I fished with an expert on the Rogue River years ago who caught fish after fish on a fly that started out as a Royal Coachman but ended up without a tail and the ball of herl at the hook's end. It looked ready for the junk heap.

The learned fly man speaks of a steelhead "riffle." That shows what he knows about it. The name may have come from the type of water the Forty-Niners panned gold in, but it is not descriptive of steelhead water. What is referred to as a riffle is a type of water—speed of water—somewhere between a rapids and a quiet pool. There is, usually, a bar or beach with shallow water on one bank and a steep bank on the other. They are easy to locate from the road that follows the rivers. The fly man wades in from the shallow side until he is almost up to his elbows to begin his fishing. He does this if the current does not knock him off his feet in the meantime. The current in this type of water has good speed. The fish will be in a certain speed of water, usually closer to the far bank.

About 40 years ago, I walked down to a bar on California's

mighty Klamath River and watched a fly fisherman fight and finally land a large fish. He said it was a steelhead. At that time, I did not know a steelhead from a carp. I had a long talk with him—he did the talking, I did the listening, and with more interest than if he had been telling me how to get rich in one easy lesson. I did get rich—rich in enjoyment and health but not in money. I told him I was a little tired from my long trip and that I would give the fishing the good old college try in the morning. I told him what equipment and tackle I had. He approved but, strangely, he did not take much interest in my flies. "If you meet me here around eight-thirty tomorrow morning, I will show you the ropes," he said. Thanking him, I went back to camp.

The next morning, decked out in chest-high stocking-foot waders, wool socks, and felt-soled wading shoes, I grabbed my 9-foot split bamboo rod equipped with a Hardy St. John reel, a 9-foot leader tapered down to a so-called eight-pound test tippet, and a Size 2 Royal Coachman and headed for the bar and my adviser.

It is necessary to explain that this fishing began before fiber glass rods were born and before Shooting Tapers were thought of. We had salt-water squidding line for backing, as I remember, and my reel held about 175 yards of backing. Casting distance in those days fell far short of what is accomplished today. Our sinking lines did not get down as fast as the HiD ones of today.

When he told me to go up to the head of the riffle, I asked him what a riffle was. "Do you want to fish or argue? Go up to where the fast water slows, wade out as far as you can, cast as far as you can—as close to the other bank as possible—and hold the rod out at right angles to the water so that when the line straightens out your fly will be a little farther out in the current. After you think the line, leader, and fly have straightened, let the fly soak for a minute and you just might get a pleasant surprise." I followed his instructions to the dot. The minute seemed like an hour, but just then something grabbed my fly and almost knocked me off my feet. My first steelhead. The system worked; man, did it work. How to estimate the time to soak the fly is not important. To give the time is. I count to 100, and that is a minute or close enough. That kind person will never know how much I appreciate his help. Using his method, I had confidence, which is so needed for successful fishing, that I could always catch steelhead in this or other typical riffles, providing, of course, that the "run was in." It may be of interest to say that although the river was full of fish, two well-equipped fly men did not get a fish in ten days. As soon as their flies even started to straighten, they picked up and made another cast. You just can't catch steelhead with the fly in the air. Some guys just do not want to be told.

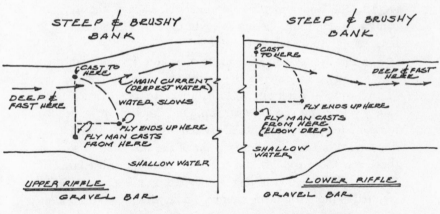

A typical steelhead riffle. A shad riffle is similar. The fly man may have to move downstream until he gets into fish. Do this slowly and thoroughly.

As the sketch illustrates, the water above the riffle is rapids—much too fast to wade. But where the man told me to enter the water was at the tail end of the rapids and was slower. The wading was difficult because of the speed of the water and the river bottom. Someone had greased each and every rock in the area. Just below my wading position, the river slowed and widened. I think that the fly drifted down to the fish, but the fish may have followed the fly and hit—after the long count—with the line, leader, and fly in the current directly below me.

In the old days, nobody got into the river at daylight: eight-thirty was the usual hour. Fishing was enjoyed until about four-thirty in the afternoon, giving a full day of casting and wading—which is enough work for anyone. On sunny days, the sun on the water had no adverse effect on the fishing, at least in the opinion of the old-timers. On cool days, any sun felt mighty good to the wader in the cold water. Nowadays, the fly man can't wait. He thinks he has to be in the water as soon as it is light enough to see where to wade.

The rotation system used to be in vogue. It went like this: The first fly man entered the water some 100 feet above the "fishy" water—water known to hold fish from experience—and slowly worked his way downstream. Once hooked up, he headed for shore to fight and eventually beach his fish. The next man in line waded out to the starting point of the first man as soon as there was room enough and followed the same procedure. By this method, the good fishing was shared by all, and it actually resulted in more fish being caught. Today this method is seldom used. Fly men are too impatient.

Knowing where the fish are in a riffle is half the battle. After a riffle has been successfully fished through once, the holding water is known, and that water is the place to fish day after day and is potentially good year after year. Sometimes on a very long riffle the fish will be in a very short stretch of it. You have to know this. If you should start fishing below this particular piece of water, you would fish your heart out and never get a strike. In a riffle new to you, go in at the head of it and prospect it slowly. However, with a fisherman below you who does not keep moving into the fish, you are just "cut off at the pass." You can offer to help the culprit get lost by any legal method. I will never forget "the little old lady from Pasadena" who waded out 10 feet in the famous Terwar riffle on the Klamath, cast into a foot of water, and retrieved her bait in 6 inches of water while I waited 2 hours to get into that part of the river. She did not catch a fish and would not have done so in a million years unless some fish felt sorry for her and was able to swim in such thin water. She was not within 100 feet of the productive water. However, her fishing license (and I assume she had one) gave her the right to fish any way and any place she wanted to. (I did try to push her into the river, but she had a very sneaky left jab.)

After 3 full seasons on the Klamath (I fished one riffle for 72 days) I heard, from an unknown source, of larger fish, easier wading, and crystal-clear water in Oregon's Rogue River. After leaving Grants Pass and driving over an unpaved road for 25 miles, I reached the Galice Ranger Station and stopped for fishing information. I was told to contact a man who, the ranger said, took time out from his mining claim to do some fly fishing. As soon as I met the man I told him I was interested in fly fishing for steelhead. I had it made. He was a giant of a man who could cast a country mile. He was hampered by using hip boots rather than chest-high waders, but he could catch fish, and under his guidance on the new, to me, riffles, I was soon enjoying steelhead fishing far superior to that found in the Klamath. The fish averaged almost twice as large, the rocks were not greased, and the water was, if not what is called gin clear, at least fairly clear. I enjoyed 12 full seasons of this man's company and the steelhead. My small umbrella tent was pitched on his mining claim. Before the weather got down to a nighttime temperature of 19 degrees, I cut a hole in the roof of the tent and installed a tin miner's stove and 10 feet of stove pipe. A few twigs warmed the tent in great style. Although fish of over 30 pounds have been taken in Canada's Kispiox River, I am sure, considering all the conditions, I had the finest fishing in the world. Each season was of 3 months' duration with only a few "days off" because of dirty water.

Big moments with steelhead are never forgotten. I have an ample supply to be savored. Such as the sunny morning I waded out up to my elbows in a riffle some 100 yards from camp, made a good cast, let the fly soak, and had a solid smash. The fish tore off downstream with my reel screaming. Just above the rapids, it made a beautiful jump. It looked to be 4 feet long, and I was really shaken. I had to follow the fish through a couple of hundred feet of fast water. I finally beached a 9-pounder—the best but not the largest steelhead I ever caught. In the next 2 hours, I landed 2 more fish—5-pounders. After some picture-taking, I gave the fish to my mailman friend who brought my grocery orders from the nearest store, 25 miles away. A morning to remember.

I remember when I helped a newcomer to his first steelhead. As soon as the fish was hooked, he developed "buck fever." As fast as I led him away from the water's edge so he could beach the fish, he ran back. Finally, he pulled the fish up on the bar, threw his rod down, and ran for the fish. He made only one mistake: He ran the wrong way. Why he did not step on his rod is a wonder. He sure had a good time, and I almost died laughing. From then on we called him "Wrong-Way Corrigan."

One morning before breakfast, I was elbow-deep in the Ranger Station riffle when I hooked into something fishy. I could not follow the fish downriver, since the water was too deep and the bank too rough. I held the fish in the current for an hour before a sheep herder boated me to the opposite bank where I fought the fish for hours, only to lose it in the rapids. It was no doubt a large salmon; at least it did not fight like a steelhead.

Early one autumn morning, a fishing companion and I hiked downriver 3 miles from the end of a road. He waded out into his favorite water, and I moved down another quarter of a mile to Tyee Bar. This was a famous piece of placer mining ground in the days of the Forty-Niners. Famous to the tune of one million dollars. It was the location of Zane Grey's cabin, or so it is said. There was not a fisherman in sight, upriver or down. The wading was tricky, since the bottom was covered with boulders. Not knowing the water, I started at the head of the riffle. Finding these fish was a snap. They must have been crowding each other because the entire riffle was productive. I would fish it from one end to the other and then start in at the head again. The fish were 5-to-7-pounders, none smaller and none larger. For the next 4 hours, I hooked fish until I ran out of steam. When I hiked back to my fishing friend, he had the same story and the fish to prove it.

These are exceptional cases, to be sure. Some days it seemed as if there were not a fish in the river. But that is steelhead fishing—then and now.

SHAD. If it is true that shad were introduced to the West Coast around 1870, it is strange they were not known to the fly man until about 1950. To the best of my knowledge, these shad were first fly-fished in the Russian River of northern California. From there fly fishermen went to the American, Feather, and Yuba rivers, in that order. The waters of the three rivers eventually reach San Francisco Bay.

Like the steelhead, shad are anadromous. They spend the greater part of their lives in salt water and ascend the free-flowing rivers of the West Coast on their spawning run. The interest fly fishermen show in this fish is increasing yearly at a very high rate. In the spring of 1969, I counted 75 fly rodders on one Yuba River riffle.

The shad season starts in early May and continues into June, depending on water conditions, which are somewhat related to weather conditions. In 1970, repairs to the gates of an upstream dam turned the water of the Yuba high and cold. This slowed the fishing. The American River is hot fishing when water comes off the top of the upstream dam, but the sport suffers when water comes through the gates at the bottom. Fishing conditions change day to day, year to year, and from river to river.

Shad come into the Klamath River, Oregon's Coos Bay, and the Umpqua River. From what I have seen of Oregon rivers, the fishing would have to be done by boaters. Conditions are not right for the wading fly man. There are, no doubt, other rivers filled—in season—with shad, but the California rivers get the big play.

Shad make an appearance in San Francisco Delta in the latter part of April and are of interest to bump netters at night. The fly men get interested—to put it mildly—when the fish appear in the riffles, the same type of water used by steelheaders. Many of my shad friends start early and stay late, each day and each season. I would, too, if I lived a little closer. The fishing is that exciting. As it is, I have fished 2-week periods for 16 years and missed only 2 seasons. The action will please anyone.

The riffles are thick with fish. There have been reports, which I believe, of over 100 shad being caught and released by one expert in a 14-hour day. Shad hit hard and fight hard in current and do some jumping. Shad are related to tarpon, which are the world's greatest jumpers. Most of the fish caught are in the 2-pound class. A 4- or 5-pounder is a great fish.

As noted, shad are found in the same type of water as steelhead—a riffle—and fly-fishing tackle, equipment, and methods are very similar. The fly pattern is different, and wading water and weather are much warmer during shad season than during the fall steelhead season. Recently, I read an article that told of fly fishing for shad on the surface, but I've never seen one caught on top. Shad are usually bottom huggers.

It is now the middle of May, and the shad are in. If you are a newcomer to this fishing and would care to join me, I will show you the ropes. Bring your 9-foot rod, a reel—with a good click or drag—holding 150 yards of backing, monofilament shooting line, and a fast-sinking single-taper line (Shooting Head) that fits the rod. A 9-foot leader, tapered down to .010-inch diameter or a size heavier and some Carl Ludemann-pattern flies in Sizes 2 to 10, weighted and unweighted, will complete the tackle. Chest-high waders, either boot-foots or stocking-foots with felt or carpet soles, will be needed for the deep wading that goes with this fishing. A landing net can be useful or you can grab the squirming fish by hand, but things get a little splashy. During crowded fishing conditions, you do not leave your hot spot to beach a fish. I will pick you up at 8 in the morning, if that's all right with you. Bring a lunch and we will make a day of it. We can fish on and off until dark.

After arriving at the parking site (it looks at times like a parking lot) we get into wading gear, pick up our tackle, and take a short walk to our fishing water. Some guys wear fishing coats covered with emblems, badges, and citations, and hats laden with flies. Then there are those who dress like farmers. I try to fool the experts by using the farmer routine. But I do wear sunglasses. A fly box and some tippet material is stashed away on the person.

Arriving at the water, we look the situation over to decide where to fish—where there is room to fish. This fishing is different from most. Here, fly fishermen crowd in on each other because of fishing pressure. No one objects if it is done in a reasonable way. Wading in just below another fly man is proper unless the wader goes out so far that he interferes with the man's fishing. My idea of heaven is to have a couple of hundred feet of

water between me and the fly man below me. It is then possible
to fish very slowly downriver until I start hitting fish. The days
that have the least fishermen are Mondays, Tuesdays, Thurs-
days, and Fridays. Wednesdays and weekends are generally
more crowded.

We wade out, avoiding any back casts from other fly men, to
line up with the others, usually elbow-deep. After getting off a
good 80-to-100-foot cast, we go into our steelhead method of
letting the fly soak. We just stand there like two bumps on a log.
But unlike two bumps on a log, we count. In cold water a count
of 2 minutes' duration is not too much. I count to 200, and that
is close to 2 minutes. It seems like an hour. If I do not get a strike
during that time, I move down a couple of feet and repeat the
process. I continue to fish this way until I run into fish or run
out of fishing space. If the man below me looks like the gangster
type I move to, say, within 20 feet of him (unless he gives me a
hard eye), but if the man looks like the understanding type, I
stop about 10 feet above him. Fishing down on a guy does not
hurt his fishing; it makes it rougher for him on his line pickup
if he is right-handed. This is the correct way to shad fish,
whether the fishing is hot or cold.

Trying to help someone enjoy this sport is not always successful. One experience comes to mind. I was into numerous
shad. Two strangers, dressed and equipped for fishing, were
looking on. When I came out of the water, I asked them how
they were doing. They told me they hadn't the slightest idea how
to fish for shad. They were well equipped, so I told them if they
would wade out to where I had been fishing, starting some 100
feet above and slowly work down, they would get into lots of
fish. I also gave them the soaking fly routine. "Let your fly soak
for at least a minute." I would like to say I helped them, but
they did not seem to go for my advice. They did not move and
they did not let the fly soak. They did not catch shad, either.

Several years ago, I was in the lineup and catching shad. The other fly rodders were also hot, with one exception. He was about 20 feet below me, so he was in sight at all times. I could plainly see what was wrong. He was casting too often and not letting the fly soak. When he asked me what fly I was using, it gave me the opportunity to "tell all." I moved down to him, cut off my fly, tied it on his leader and told him to go to it, with the added advice on fly-soaking. He followed instructions. Soon, a shad grabbed his fly and tried to take his rod away. That was his first shad. He was tickled pink and so was I. From then on, he was a good shad man.

I first heard of shad fishing 18 years ago. California's Russian River was the place. A man was out on a riffle near Guerneville, catching fish after fish. It looked great. I went up to a fly man on the bank—he was probably resting from the fast action—and that is when I got the word on Shooting Heads for the first time. "You'll need this type of line if you're ever going to reach the fish." It seemed that the good fishing was accomplished by casting a mile or thereabouts to the opposite bank. So, into a tackle store. I was soon equipped with the long-distance outfit. But something was wrong. My casting was poor. Finally it was discovered that the wrong line had been put in the right box. Upon getting the right line, my casting improved. Still I could not reach far enough on that particular riffle, so I moved upstream and found water with fish closer in.

I next tried the Feather River, but there was little excitement there; I went scouting. Driving along Highway 20 East and stopping off at a roadside cafe, I heard of some fishing on the Yuba River, adjacent to the highway. I discovered what turned out to be one of finest shad rivers in California, if not the U.S.A. I had this fishing to myself for several years, but keeping secrets is not one of my strong points, and the word spread to my fishing friends. I feel like the grand old man of the Yuba. The river has held up well in spite of fishing pressure—some 1000 fly men strong.

One year, I got up on the Yuba early in the season, before I began relying on scouting reports. The manager of the motel where I stopped told me that his 2 boys were shad fishermen. He said there was not a fish in the river. The next morning, having nothing better to do, I went to my favorite riffle and, by using the long count, caught a lot of nice shad. The water was cold. I did not get a fish before the count of 100. Most were caught closer to the 200 count. Two game wardens came by and told me they did not believe their eyes. "There are no fish in the river," one informed me.

Last shad season, there was some repair work being done on the gates of a dam some 30 miles upriver. The water was high and cold most of the season. But one day, for some reason, the water was down and I was able to wade across the river and get to the next upstream riffle. This riffle was a narrow one, and with a little wading I could toss the fly into shallow water at the opposite bank. I was using a fast-sinking line, and all I did was hook up on the bottom until I remembered a remark I overheard: "When fishing shallow water with a fast-sinking line, start retrieving fast as soon as the fly goes under." I used this method, and I had shad fishing like I have never experienced. The shad hit this fast-moving fly almost as soon as it went under. They fought like steelhead and jumped like crazy. A most interesting day, brought on mainly because I keep my ears flapping when anyone, regardless of his experience or lack of it, talks fishing.

BONITO (Shore Fishing). The Pacific bonito range the West Coast from the Mexican border to British Columbia. The ones we are concerned with range the shoreline between San Diego and Redondo Bay, California. Schools of these fish move in irregular schedules. They are where you find them. The shore-caught fish are mostly in the 2-pound class and are great fighters.

The fishing season usually starts in late December and lasts for several months. As I am writing this—in the middle of December—I am not getting any reports of any local fishing. When the fishing starts, the phone starts ringing. The year 1968 was a banner year, but in 1969 the fish had a different schedule, and many fly men were disappointed. This fish often takes up the slack in winter fly fishing.

It was nearly daylight one cool morning when I arrived at the jetty at San Diego's Mission Bay. As I headed for my favorite rock, I heard a voice from the darkness. "Hi, Sam, what held you up?" All my life, I have had to contend with smart alecks. However, not to be outdone, I answered, "How is the old commercial fisherman?" This is a dig at the boys who use a 2-fly rig. They often catch 2 fish at a time.

I stick with one fly on the leader in order to get more distance. Maybe I should learn to cast. There is no doubt that the 2-fly rig attracts the fish better. After one fish is hooked, there is, usually, a follower to grab the second fly. Two fish at a time gets a little complicated when they come into the rocks during the landing process, however.

Since the first hour of daylight accounts for the best fishing of the day, many poor old working stiffs can get into hot fishing before the whistle blows—before they have to head for the Steel Works. Just think of it, they get fish and a paycheck on the same day.

Standard salt-water fly-fishing rigs are used. Lighter tackle would provide more sport, but at a sacrifice in distance that is so important. The marabou streamer in Size 4 and the baby popper in Size 6 are favorites. A 9-foot leader tapering to .010 inch is used. One- and 2-piece rods made up from Fenwick-Grizzly No. 1083 blanks, Conolon blanks, Lamiglas blanks, Ferrulites such as the FF 98 and Scientific Anglers, Inc., No. 10 system rods are favorites. A single taper (Shooting Head) line is a must for the fishing. A floating head can be used for both the streamer and the popper, because these fish hit at or near the surface. I think the popper is more successful. It certainly provides more sport.

The streamer type flies have little standard. They are used in all colors, all sizes, and of all materials known to fly tiers. There is no hook standard. Bonito, when hungry—and they usually are at daybreak—might hit anything flylike that moves. To pin it down to one fly, I would use a No. 4 Jamison barbless hook. The pattern, the marabou special, about 2 inches long.

Some San Diego anglers prefer streamer flies to poppers. A Wet Cel 2 head is used. This line seems to work better a little later in the morning, when the fish go down a little deeper. I fished with one of the streamer advocates—a man with over 50 years of fishing experience. My poppers were better at first, but he caught up with me and soon surpassed me.

Felt or carpet soles are needed. The rocks are usually wet and slippery. Winter mornings, even in Southern California, are nippy, and warm clothing is necessary.

There are times when bonito are more interested in lunch than breakfast. One noontime, I was parked at a tidal bay and, having an hour to kill, I thought I would get in some casting practice. My rod was rigged with a Size 6 marabou popper. On my first cast, a bonito clobbered the bug. On my next 9 casts I picked up 7 fish. This was, of course, a matter of luck, not experience. I just happened on a school of hungry fish. The Size 6 hook-gap left nothing to be desired. Every fish was solidly hooked. The fish were still hitting when I had to leave. That kind of fishing makes any fly man what is known as an expert.

So, if you are near any shore-type bonito, it is well worth a try. Make a good cast with either a streamer or popper, and retrieve. The speed of the retrieve does not seem to be too important. I do all right with a slow retrieve. However, if you see the fish following your offering without hitting, pull in line with all the speed possible. This sometimes brings results. Don't worry about being too fast for a bonito—it can't be done.

There is nothing more stubborn, at times, than a fly-fishing nut. One day I was fishing near a half-completed marina at Redondo Bay, California, with the strict resolution that I was going to catch bonito on a popper or else. I threw that popper out all day. A half-dozen fish would follow the popper in to shore on each cast, staying about 12 inches below it. I tried various speeds of retrieve, but no soap, not one strike. I fished the day with no success, slept in my van in a parking lot and, the next morning, went with the popper again. Finally, I got a fish and headed for home. It might have been a different story if I had been using a streamer. Maybe not. All the time I was not catching fish, the lure-and-bait boys also were not catching fish.

But that's fishing, so find a nice flat rock surrounded by bonito and have a go at 'em.

OFFSHORE BONITO. My first experience with offshore bonito was not as successful as it might have been. A free-lance writer, having heard of some good fly fishing in the kelp beds off the San Diego coast, invited 6 members of the local fly-fishing club on a charter-type boat to get material for his article.

When the boat's skipper found the fish, the anchor went down. The stampede to the stern was something to see. Just about then, I realized that I should have stayed in bed. There were two things wrong with the picture. Someone should have been in charge of that motley bunch of fly men. In the second place, the boat was suitable for a group of bait fishermen but not right for space-consuming fly rodders.

Under the conditions, the stern was no place for the man who prefers to be a live coward to a dead hero. I got out of there and headed for the bow. I started out with a Size 4 popper. A 75-foot cast was needed. At that distance, I got into bonito like crazy. A crewman gaffed my first fish, and on removing the hook broke it off at the bend. I found this out a little later—after having hit after hit but no hookups. I was trying to hook fish without a hook, which is a good trick if done. The skipper, with years of experience in taking out fishing parties, told me that he had never seen so much activity as I was getting.

On another occasion, a writer invited four of us so-called fly-fishing hot-shots on a chartered U-drive boat. His knowledge of fishfinding was not too good. If he had headed up the coast and found some sport-fishing boats in action, it might have been a really good trip. To top it off, the bait tank pump went haywire, so chumming—to bring up the fish—was impossible. The writer has my sympathy—that boat cost him a bundle.

One morning, a fishing editor took me out on a sport-fishing boat. He had the camera, I was the lone fisherman, and the skipper ran the boat, chummed, and was ready with the gaff. The fish were found—they were boiling at the stern—and I went to work. It was not easy casting—the boat railing was too high, and the boat itself was what I call a roller. The fishing was hot. I had a hookup on every cast, but the 2-hour trip resulted in one fish being landed. It was 2 weeks later when I solved the mystery of so many strikes and so few fish landed. I found a fly in an old fishing shirt. It was a true barbless hook fly—no hump or twist of any kind. That fly was the one I had been using. With ocean casting there is always some slack shooting line on the deck. When a fish is hooked, this slack must be put back on the reel in order to play the fish properly. Any slack line at this time allows the fish to spit out a true barbless hook. If I had known that I was using this type of hook, I could have kept more pressure on the fish and landed most if not all of them. However, the editor got some good pictures and a good story.

My most successful trips have been as a guest of a know-it-all fly fisherman. The La Jolla, California, kelp beds was the scene.

The fishing was, at times, fantastic—a hookup a cast. At times it was so good that we would try to take the fly or popper away from the fish, but without much success. The bonito is a speedster. I have had some hot fishing in my time but this was more like a fisherman's dream than actual fishing. Granted, this kind of fishing happened to us only about 70 percent of the time, and it took some cruising to find the fish. But what more can a fly man ask? As my friend remarked, "It sure spoils you for shore-fishing bonito."

The fish average much larger out in the blue water. My best fish, so far, is a 7-pounder. A bonito of that size is a lot of fish on a fly rod. Bonito have been caught by bait fishermen in the 12-pound class. When this happens to a fly man, he will have a long battle he will not forget.

As noted, a 2-rod setup—for each fisherman—should be carried if there is space available—horizontal space. Storing a rod vertically will cause casting problems. One rod is rigged with a floating head and a Size 4 or 6 popper, and the other rod is rigged with a sinking head and a 2½-inch-long streamer fly. A floating head can be used throughout, especially if some weighted flies are at hand. My only reason for not fishing a popper at all times is that there may be a yellowtail or two under the bonito. A 9-foot leader tapered down to .012 or .0135 inch is used. The fly-rod outfit is whatever you want to use for salt-water fishing.

PACIFIC MACKEREL. The Pacific mackerel is found off the Southern California coast. One 2 feet long is considered large, and one of 5 pounds, heavy. Getting into a school of these fish results in some fast action. They do not make long runs, but they are noted for their tugging power.

One summer morning (and summertime is the season for most of the salt-water fish) I was aboard a 16-foot Boston Whaler. My son was the skipper, but he and my grandson were not equipped for this type of fishing. They brought down trolling rods from their Monterey salmon fishing. Can you think of any-thing more outlandish than using small streamer flies on heavy trolling tackle? We got into an acre of mackerel, but trolling was not the answer—not the best answer. If they had been equipped with fly-rod outfits and had been able to cast a fly line—even a short one—we would have anchored in the middle of the big school and caught fish and more fish. Mackerel seems to be one of the salt-water varieties that is better suited to fly casting than trolling.

On another occasion, I got into a school of these fish, and all was going well until a boat ran through the school and put the fish down. Boat traffic is a problem at times, especially on week-ends. Everybody and his brother gets into the act. And some of the actors don't act nice at all.

Pacific mackerel are fished for in the same manner as other salt-water fish. Chumming is helpful, and your salt-water fly tackle will do the job. A streamer fly is used. A marabou fly on a Size 2 or 4, tied on a No. 711SS or similar hook, will get the fish. A fly about 2 inches long is suggested.

PACIFIC BARRIES. The Pacific barracuda, like other bar-racuda, are long, slender fish with a mouthful of sharp teeth. They usually are not over four feet long and not over 10 to 12 pounds. Their teeth murder a monofilament leader tippet.

From my experiences with them in bays, I would say that evening fishing is preferred. The bay fish are not more than 18 inches long and do not put up much of a struggle. But they are worth fishing for, especially as a new experience and a winter pastime. One evening I got into a small school of these fish and landed and released 5 of them in a hurry.

There is a limit on these fish. Only 2 barracuda under 28 inches can be kept. When I saw a boy with a string of these un-dersized fish I asked him if he knew the ruling. He said, "They don't do anything to us kids." It seems to me that the law is a

23. Author with a nice curve in the fly rod.

24. Author landing a nice bonito in La Jolla, California, kelp beds.
Dr. Albert C. Funk.

25. A fishing friend with a striped bass from San Francisco Bay. Not large as stripers go, but nice on fly tackle. *Sam Nix.*

26. Author with a 6-pound bonito caught in the La Jolla, California, kelp beds. *Dr. Albert C. Funk.*

27. Fly man just about elbow deep in a shad riffle. *Sam Nix.*

28. Shad caught in California's Yuba River. *Sam Nix.*

29. Two school-size yellowtail from the La Jolla, California, kelp beds. The fish were caught by casting and not by trolling. Few fly men have caught these fish (north of the Mexican border) by casting. *Jeff Crowson.*

30. A young fishing companion—a purist—with 2 shore-caught bonito from San Diego's Mission Bay. *Sam Nix.*

31. Author hooked up to a Yuba River shad.

32. A fishing companion with a nice shad from California's Yuba River. *Sam Nix.*

33. Author with a sierra mackerel in San Carlos Bay, Mexico.

34. A nice Mexican toro (jack crevelle) caught on a popper at Topolobampo Bay. Note poppers used. *Sam Nix*.

35. Trigger fish caught on a sunken streamer in San Carlos Bay, Mexico. NOTE: This was the first trigger fish ever caught on a fly, to my knowledge. *Sam Nix.*

36. Author fishing for sierra mackerel at New Kino, Mexico.

37. Jim Green of Fenwick/Sevenstrand turned this 35–40-pound tarpon free unharmed. *Bernard "Lefty" Kreh, Miami, Florida.*

little lax here. It is my thought that if youngsters were made to understand that the law is for everyone, they might grow up to have a little more respect for fishing laws—and for laws in general. The boy did not resent my remarks. He and I are the best of friends.

Salt-water fly-fishing tackle is used for barries. The line, a fast-sinking single taper. The shore fishing is usually from a jetty. There are problems. You make as long a cast as possible, and retrieve. No expert can do more. The fishing is similar to shore bonito fishing, but it is a mystery why bonito and barracuda are not caught at the same time. At least I never saw it happen. It is also strange why bay fishing is better in the winter and offshore fishing better in the summer.

Offshore barracuda come in all sizes. The large ones are called log barracuda and are of interest to the fly man only as to how large a fish he can catch. And he will not land many with the standard monofilament leader. The tippet should be of wire—single-strand wire. These fish are the only ones I know of on the West Coast that do require wire. This isn't to say that monofilament will not work at times. But not as a general rule.

I got into the "logs" once. I did pretty well. I only lost every other fly on them. I did come up with one over 7 pounds. In a picture, the fish looks half the length of the fly rod and twice as thick. They put up a dragging fight and cannot be compared to a bonito for excitement.

On one trip to the kelp beds, I got into small barracuda and lost every fly I had in the box. No other fish were caught during the barracuda run. Next time I will take a nap until the school goes by.

I was using my salt-water rod and reel, an HiD fast-sinking single-taper line, shooting line, a 9-foot leader, and a 2½-inch-long marabou fly, Size 2. A fly tied on a Size 2, 6 extra-long shank hook with a tail of bucktail hair or marabou filaments tied in at the bend of the hook and nothing else might be a good fly for these sharp-toothed rascals. They could do their chewing on the bare shank.

YELLOWTAIL. About 45 years ago, a friend—some friend! —took me out on a sport-fishing boat. It was bait fishing for yellowtail, a very popular game fish found off the West Coast from the La Jolla kelp beds south into Mexico. The average size is about 20 pounds. They range in size from 4 pounds to slightly more than 50.

We soon got into fish. My best fish was a 25-pounder. All the way home I cussed this friend for getting me into so much work—and work it is, even with the heavy tackle used. I tell myself I want no part of a yellowtail over 12 pounds or so, but I do not really believe it. However, a big yellowtail on fly tackle would take hours to land (if it did not break off on kelp). But fly fishing for these fish up to 12 pounds would be real fishing.

Several years ago, I was hooked up to my first yellowtail by casting with fly tackle. I thought I was in control. For some impossible reason, the backing was caught between the spool and the frame, however. The backing can't possibly do that: It did. (It had no effect on the casting.) The fish took off in a burst of speed. When it came to the jambed backing—pow, the fish was gone, trailing my fly, leader, Shooting Head—a new one, shooting line, and yards of new backing. My fishing companion saw the fish take the fly and told me I'd lost a 12-pounder.

One evening last summer the phone rang. I answered, hoping it was a fly fisherman interested in going a couple of rounds on the interesting subject. I was real lucky. "Hi, Sam, there are reports of school yellowtail at the La Jolla kelp beds. You've been interested in getting a yellow on a fly, so how about going out with me tomorrow morning?" While the caller was saying "going out" I was saying "I would like that."

I met my fly-fishing friend at the landing ramp at 7:00 A.M. His boat was launched (mainly by his efforts), and we headed out. The first stop was at the bait receiver to pick up a scoop of chumming bait. (It is easy to ignore the use of bait to fish with, since we are so dedicated to fly fishing.) It was a 6-mile run to the fishing grounds. By "fishing grounds" I mean any old place where there might be some fishing. That means keeping an eye peeled for birds or fish. When any activity is seen, or even imagined, the streamer or popper goes out for some trolling to locate the fish. We do not, however, consider trolling as fly fishing. It does help to locate the fish. We slowly troll—as slowly as possible—the fly or popper some 100 feet off the stern while we scan the water in all directions for fish signs.

My friend got the first strike and remarked that it felt like a yellowtail. It was—a school fish of 5 pounds. It put up a great scrap. I got my camera into action. When things calmed down, I noticed a disturbance in the water some 60 feet off my side of the boat—my private territory. I got a little excited, since it did not appear to be bonito. I made a cast to the spot and retrieved without results. But the second cast was a different story. I was hooked up to a yellowtail. The fish went away from me in a hurry. After two long runs and a dogfight, I landed a 6-pound fish. The size of the fish was not remarkable. It was what is known as school yellowtail—the small ones. However, few yellowtail of any size are caught by casting a fly. Not that it is a feat of skill, but, rather, luck in finding them on or near the surface and hungry. Needless to say, I credit my host with my success. He got me to the fish. That made it a big day for me—the first yellowtail I ever landed on a fly rod.

I was using one of my 9-foot salt-water rods, an HiD head, 20-pound-class monofilament shooting line, 225 yards of backing on a Scientific Anglers, Inc., 10-system reel—a 3⅞-inch size, a 9-foot tapered leader to a .0135-inch tippet and a 3-inch marabou streamer tied on a Size 1, No. 711SS Herters hook.

When 6-to-8-inch sardines were plentiful, they were a more popular bait than the smaller anchovies. Perhaps a 6-inch fly would work better than one 3 inches long. It would be worth a try. It would mean a little less distance in casting—maybe quite a little—but yellowtail often come close to the boat. It has been said that yellowtail, on their trip up from Mexican waters, get educated, and by the time they reach offshore La Jolla, they are not too easy to hook. Bait fishermen have learned this and use very small hooks and 12- or 15-pound test line to overcome the educated fish.

At times, yellowtail roam under bonito, so I would suggest a lead-core head to get the fly down to the yellows before the bonito get it.

All salt and brackish water should be prospected by the fly rodder. The results are sometimes surprisingly good.

For example, let's take a look at San Diego's Mission Bay and the Mission Valley flood control waters, which are salty from the tides coming in and going out of Mission Bay. There are many such bays along the West Coast with a fish potential.

SPOTTED BASS. Several years ago, I prospected for spotted bass in the bay. Where I fished is a recreational beach in the summertime. In the winter it is almost deserted. With waders, I found that I could get into weed beds during the low water. And that is where fish hang out.

I was using my salt-water rod and reel with an HiD single-tapered line, a 7½-foot tapered leader, and a white fly about 1½ inches long. The wing was white bucktail hair, since this fishing was in my premarabou days.

All I know about prospecting—fish, that is—is to cast as far as possible and retrieve until the butt of the leader hits the rod's top. On this day, the results were good. I landed a half dozen spotted bass. Most of them took the fly when I had retrieved it almost all the way in. I lost some big fish, which may have been spotted bass. The fish I landed were just over the legal minimum of 12 inches.

Retrieving in this manner means a lot of line in the weedy water and some tangles. Maybe a "shooting type" basket would be useful here.

SAND BASS. The local flood control channel provided good fly fishing for sand bass. At times these bass can be seen cruising along the rocky shore, and they will take a fly avidly. Once they feel the hook, though, they head for the rocks and break off. They may be cruising along looking for crabs. They are also caught in the middle of the channel—not rocky, just weedy. Just before dark seems to be the best time for fly fishing. They are fished for at night with bait, but fly fishing in the dark is not too enjoyable.

Either a floating or sinking head can be used. And a 2-inch marabou on a 9-foot leader with a .012-inch tippet is about right. However, I saw some fish working that I did not catch. More experimenting is in order. Maybe a 3½- or 4-inch fly of the shrimp type would bring more success.

CALICO BASS. As noted, the flood control channel is salt water. The water, depending on the stage of the tide, pours in through the rocks. The fish come in through the openings to spawn. This is usually in May and early June.

One afternoon, I waded out from the south side of the channel so that I could cast toward the opposite shore. The tide was about half in, and water was pouring through the rocks, forming a river. The water was loaded with calicos. They were splashing along the rocky bank and loading up on small crabs. A fly cast close to the bank and just starting downstream would be clobbered by the fish. It was fast fishing. I got 20 of these fish in the one-pound class as fast as I could land one and make another cast.

Either a floating head or a sinking head will work under these conditions. A 1¾-inch white fly did the job. A 70-foot cast was required, so fly tackle is needed that will accomplish this. Chest-high waders are needed for comfortable fishing.

I returned to this fishing the next afternoon with the same results. On the third day, the skin divers got into the water and slowed me to a standstill.

This is just another example of finding some good fly fishing that few fishermen know about; and to the best of my knowledge, it is known by few fly men.

Calicos are found in deep water off the coast, but this means fishing in kelp. On one trip, we were at anchor with a bait tank loaded with dead bait. I would make a cast, lean the rod against the transom, throw in some dead bait, and come up with some calicos. They were hitting my dead fly.

Fish caught in fairly shallow water of bays and channels seem to put up a better battle for their size than those caught in deep water. They seem to run closer to the surface and cannot head for deep water and dog it.

STRIPED BASS. Striped bass is a well-known sea bass that was successfully transplanted to the West Coast. It is a fine food fish. It grows to over 100 pounds. It is another anadromous fish, living the greater part of its life in salt water and making its spawning runs up fresh-water streams. The West Coast striped bass fishing seems limited to San Francisco Bay in California and two waters in Oregon: Coos Bay and the Umpqua River.

October is considered the best month for fly fishing in San Francisco Bay, and June the time to fish in Oregon. The early morning—the first hour of daylight, and the evenings—until it gets too dark for the fly man, are the best fishing times.

There is some wading water in the Carquinas Straits of San Francisco Bay. There is a lot of wading water in Coos Bay but, in general, the fishing is done from a boat. A 16-footer with a 10-horsepower motor is recommended as a minimum. Bay waters can kick up pretty good, especially in the afternoons. This is especially true in San Francisco Bay.

Taking stripers on fly tackle is exciting fishing. You can hang a whale of a fish. The fishing is usually successfully done when stripers are found breaking the surface in their chase for bait fish such as anchovies. From my experience, surface feeding is not found often—not nearly often enough—by the fly rodder. Striper water is loaded with grass shrimp, making it mandatory to fish the fly just off the bottom—not a very interesting way to fly fish, at least not until a good fish is hooked. Then it is a bit of all right.

A husky fly rod, a reel with lots of backing, and a Shooting Head are needed. The stage of the tide governs the kind of fly line to use. If the tide is strong, a fast-sinking line such as the HiD or a faster-sinking line—the lead core—is needed. If the fish are surfacing, a large popper on a floating head might be more suitable. It would provide a lot more fun. But to me, a popper should be used when the water is quiet—at the top or the bottom of the tide, if wind is not a factor.

The fly to use is more a matter of length than color. This is the advice given me by the man who probably knows more about fly fishing for stripers, especially in San Francisco Bay, than anyone. He also told me that a 4-inch fly was about right in October. He uses flies as long as 7 inches. A leader tippet of about .0135 inch (12-pound class) on a heavy-butted, 9-foot leader is suitable.

Chest-high boot-foot waders with felt or carpet soles, a wading staff for any dirty water, and warm clothes may be needed. If there is such a thing as an up-to-date chart for the waters you intend to fish, it will give you an idea of how deep you may have to go with the streamer. It will also determine how far you can wade. Every additional foot of wading distance makes for better fishing.

Prospecting unknown water is difficult. I hit Coos Bay in July

1968. The manager of the motel suggested the north shore along the dike road leading to the paper mill. On the way, I met an old-time resident who showed me the water—what was considered good striper water.

The tide was going out when I started to fish—my first try for stripers. It was easy wading water, and things looked good. I called on my steelhead and shad experience. The water was a riffle at that time. I was using an HiD Shooting Taper line, a 9-foot leader tapering to .012 inch, and a marabou fly on a Size 4, 3 extra-long shank hook—a fly about 2½ inches over-all.

I had not made many casts before I got a terrific strike. The line melted off the reel with the fish heading for the far bank. I hung on for dear life, and then the hook pulled out. It must have been a monster. I came out of the water, sat on the bank, and cried my eyes out. To lose the first striper I ever hooked was heartbreaking. As I am writing about it, I notice a tear or two sliding down my rosy cheeks.

I fished hard and long for three days without success. I like to think that it was a case of not enough fish in the area. I waded a mile of that water, several times, covering all the water within range of some good long casts. I saw only one striper at work. Maybe a larger fly would have produced. Maybe I should have tried after-dark fishing.

On the north side of the dike road is a square mile of water at high tide. At low tide it is a sand flat cut by several channels. It is fished at low tide by walking along the edges of channels looking for fish activity. It is like bonefishing: more hunting than fishing. The fishing is not the blind type. If I am ever there with more available fish around, I will stay until the run is over, whether it is weeks or months.

The lower Umpqua River, from where the bridge crosses the river on Highway 101 to the ocean, is considered the area to fly fish. Once the stripers get upstream of that area, on their spawning run, the fishing is for trollers and bait fishermen. The lower river is considered boating water, but it looks wadable in places. It also looks as if the wading would be in mud.

In early October of 1969, a fishing companion and I tried to rent a 16-foot outboard at Rodeo in California's San Pablo Bay. The boat was available but without a motor. We had to use the cartop—a 12-footer with a 5-horsepower kicker. There was no launching ramp. We had to slide the boat down a steep bank and drag it over a wide beach. We wound up the motor and made the short run to the Brothers—a couple of small islands close to shore. It is a well-known striper spot with strong current that stripers go for. I caught my first striper, at long last. It was 22 inches long. A little later, I caught his twin brother. No great size for stripers, but about then I would have settled for a 6-incher. The fishing was by casting from the anchored boat. We also tried trolling the fly when drifting. I was using a fast-sinking head, and my friend was trolling a lead-core head. He picked up 5 fish—his best an 8-pounder, which sure looked big to me. I got one bite. It was from a yellowjacket when I stepped on shore. This—not the yellowjacket—leads me to believe I was not fishing deep enough. It will lead you to believe that my friend is the better fisherman. His parting words were, "Sam, if you keep at it, someday you will be a fly fisherman."

The fly man's goal is stripers working on the surface within casting range. One morning at daylight we were just coming off the west end of San Rafael Bridge in the Bay area when we spotted working fish close enough to reach from shore. It looked great until we noticed the no-parking-anywhere signs. By the time we found a parking place and walked back, the fish were not in sight.

Fishing stripers with fly tackle (or any other tackle, for that matter) is a little discouraging. Most of the fly rodders I know in the San Francisco area do not talk it up much. However, if I lived in the area, I would work at it. Stripers run large, and I like to land large fish.

SALTON SEA CORVINA. Although the Salton Sea in California's Imperial Valley is miles away from the ocean, it is salty. It is 300 square miles of fish. One of these is the corvina— a transplant from Mexico's Gulf of California, or, if you prefer, the Sea of Cortez.

Several years ago, I drove to Salton Sea to prospect corvina. A sandy road, off the east shore Highway 111, led to the "Salt Works." It is where the "Salt Works" used to be located. I could see a couple of what appeared to be telephone poles sticking out of the water. The poles have long since been removed because of the hazard to boaters, especially the after-dark type. And the sandy road was closed because of litterbugs. It is possible to walk to the area from the state park at the Niland marina. It is considered a good fishing area.

The water is shallow, and I could wade out 200 feet or more on hard sand bottom. I fished and I fished. I finally connected with 2 18-inch corvina.

I was using a salt-water fly-fishing outfit with a fast-sinking Shooting Head, a 9-foot leader tapered to .012 inch, and a 2-inch bucktail streamer fly. Chest-high waders were worn, although the water was warm enough to fish wet.

The season for the fishing would be in the spring, when the water and the air warm, and in the fall. It is just too hot in the the summertime and too cold in the wintertime for pleasant fishing. I do not know that there is any special time in the day for best fishing.

On another trip to this fishing area, two of us left home in the evening and arrived at the sea in the dark. We tested the water. It was quite warm. We camped out on the sand, and the next morning at daylight we got into waders and went fishing. My friend, a master of the fly rod, worked the water to the south, and I headed north. We did a good job in covering the water but not in catching fish. I was using a 4-inch popper on a floating head, and my companion was using a 2-inch streamer on a sinking head. One swirl at the popper was it. I have no doubt that we were in fish.

On another occasion, I waded out in the same area—off the Niland marina. The fish were thick. They were bumping into me. For all the good I did, I should have brought a landing net instead of fly tackle. The shore fishermen, using bait, were having a poor time, also. There is a lot of bait in the water but, with more prospecting, I think that the corvina could be caught in good numbers.

On my next trip to the water, I will have a supply of streamers in sizes 3 to 6 inches long. And I will fish the streamers on the bottom regardless of the depth of the water. As will be noted, corvina in the Gulf of California can be taken easily on poppers or streamers. The fishing could depend, of course, on the amount of feed in the water. It could also depend on the mood of the fish.

At times, the fish are in shallow water, which is ideal for the wading fly man. When the fish are in deep water a boat is, of course, required. The boater should realize that the Salton Sea can get rough—really rough.

For the fly man who lives close to the Salton Sea, it calls for some experimenting. If the correct method and the right fly are found, he would have wonderful fishing. It is worth a try.

THE PACIFIC SEA TROUT. The Pacific sea trout is a relative of the white sea bass (a Pacific croaker) and the weakfish of the Atlantic coast. The sea trout, the white sea bass, and the weakfish—the unspotted variety—are similar in shape, in coloration, and finwise. They are members of a family of temperate- and warm-water fish that frequent flats and bays. The Pacific sea trout does not seem to range the Pacific Coast any great distance above the Mexican border. San Diego's Mission Bay seems to be the extent of their northern run. It is a great fish and certainly deserves the attention of the fly rodder, if and where found.

A few winters ago, I was casting my arm off for bonito in Quivera Basin in San Diego when a fish took my streamer and tried to make it to the open ocean in one long, sizzling run. My reel almost turned inside out. I knew I was hooked into something more than the average 2-pound bonito. I finally landed a 6-pound sea trout. This is one of the largest trout ever caught locally and is the only one caught by a fly fisherman that I have heard of—and I know I would have heard. With a small boat, the fly man could fish near the bait barge in the basin, with a good chance of success. Wintertime is most productive. They are, however, considered a year-round fish.

I was using a one-piece rod, assembled with a Fenwick-Grizzly No. FF 1083 blank—a 9-footer. The Hardy Princess reel was a little small, with too weak a click, for my idea of sea trout fishing. A No. 10 Shooting Taper HiD line with 20-pound-class monofilament was on the reel. One hundred yards of backing was all the small reel would hold. The fly line had been shortened 2 feet at the butt end to better match the rod's action. The weight was cut from 300 grains to about 275 grains. The marabou fly was 2 inches over-all and tied to a Size 4, 3 extra-long shank, regular wire hook. The heavy-butted, 9-foot leader tapered down to .012 inch. The so-called "no good" Turle knot stayed tight.

TRANSPLANTED ATLANTIC SALMON. The Atlantic salmon was transplanted in Hosmer Lake, formally called Mud Lake. Suttle Lake also contains these fish. The lakes are located near Century Drive out of Bend, Oregon. Hosmer is a barbless hook, release-all-fish deal. Suttle Lake is not.

Most of the fishing is done by a fly man casting from a standing position in a boat with a man at the oars. The boat is slowly rowed along the shoreline, some 60 feet out, with the caster covering a lot of water. Another good bet at Hosmer is to have a boat and kicker to fish the upper end of the lake where there is little traffic. This is also where the large brook trout hang out.

Your pet dry fly is needed for this fishing. A long rod is popular. Something in the 8½-to-9-foot class. A weight forward floating line and a 9-to-12-foot leader tapered to a fine tippet for the 14 and 16 dry flies are needed. I started out with Blue Duns in Size 16 and ended with Brown Hackles in Size 14. It is suggested that you check locally for other favorites.

The season for the fishing is as soon as the lake is opened, before the water warms and the fish go down, and in the fall when the water cools and the fish are again interested in surface stuff.

In early 1967, I made arrangements to meet one of my fishing friends at Hosmer. This former world-champion caster would show me how it was done. His help would have been invaluable, but he was detoured by his company to a casting exhibition. I would be on my own.

Some nice guy, hearing that I was headed for the lake, sent me a dozen Blue Duns in Size 16. When I looked at the flies, I wondered what I was in for. I hadn't used a fly that small in 40 years.

When I arrived at the lake, I was glad I had brought my pram. The lake is too brushy for much shore fishing and too deep to wade out past the brush line. I launched the pram and solved the problem. So far so good, but my 7½-foot dry fly rod was a little short for casting at a sitting position in the small boat. I could, of course, have stood up to cast, but at the risk of going overboard. It was the only dry fly rod I had. I would row some 50 feet out from the brush and cast toward shore. The fish were in a jolly mood and hit my dry fly, but I had too many strikes and not enough hookups. It seems that a Size 16 fly hook in the Jamison barbless type has the pig's tail barb too close to the eye (the eye of the hook, not the eye of the pig). I was missing too many fish.

I found some Size 14 hooks of 1 extra-long shank, 1 extra-light wire, and with a turned-up eye. I flattened the barb and tied up some Brown Hackles with the only material I had at hand. I was now in business. I also caught salmon on a 2-inch-long marabou streamer.

I lost a lot of flies—by trying to remove the hook while the fish were flopping in the water—from breakage of the fine tippet. Netting the fish is frowned on.

A fish specialist at the lake told me I was catching the 9-inch salmon that had been stocked the year before. They had planted 5000 salmon, and I was catching these stocked fish. They had grown to 18 inches in one year. I landed 2 fish 24 inches long.

When I met the man who recommended the fishing, I told him it did not result in much excitement. He told me he had fished the lake the year before and the fish were much larger and were terrific fighters. One of my fishing companions reached the lake 2 days after I left. The next time I saw him, he said he was not too impressed with the fishing. Maybe the water was warm and the fish were sluggish.

CHINOOK SALMON. Fly fishing for Chinook (king) salmon is gaining in popularity. The Smith River of northern California is a favorite place for this action. Although I am not writing from personal experience, the information is authentic.

October and November are considered the best months. Before going to the river, weather conditions should be checked. Rain will put a damper on the fishing. However, the Smith clears in a few days once the rain stops and then is usually hot fishing.

A pram or other small cartop boat is used by most of the fly boys—usually one man to a boat. The eager beavers get out on the water at their favorite locations as soon as it is light enough to see. Some even launch their boats in the dark.

The flies are tied on Mustad No. 7970, or similar, in sizes 2 and 4. The 5 extra-strong wire hook has hollow points, but because of the heavy wire are a little coarse and need some touching up, or so the hook catalog states. The brown shrimp pattern

used has been described. Of course, it is always a logical idea to
talk to the fly men who are having success. There is more than
one pattern. A tippet of .012 or .0135 inch is favored.

Lead core line is used as a Shooting Head—the maximum
weight the rod will handle. A tapered leader about 9 feet long
should be satisfactory. Fly rods used are as short as 8 feet.

Fly-caught salmon range from 10 to well over 30 pounds.
These fish put up a long, hard fight and may have to be fol-
lowed. Before you start fishing you had better have your
Wheaties.

There is a boat rental and trailer park near the small town of
Smith River. It is about a quarter of a mile upriver from the
mouth. Boats may have to be reserved ahead of time and
guides may be advisable for the newcomer for this special type of
fly fishing. The most productive fishing is some 4 or 5 miles upriver from Trails End—the boat rental-trailer park. The
Elite Motel in Crescent City is roughly 15 miles from the fishing and is used as headquarters by many fly men. The manager
of the motel will help you with information on the fishing and
will contact guides. Salmon Harbor resort also supplies guides
and is located near the mouth of the river.

There may be some wading water. It may be practical to row
to some wading water, anchor the boat, and fish by wading. To
most fly men, wading is the "only way to fly." Boat fishing,
most of us feel, is never done unless absolutely necessary.

There are some jack salmon up to 5 pounds in the river at
salmon time. I caught jacks in the Klamath River, near the
mouth, years ago on a Size 8 black fly. There may be some steelheading downriver from Jed Smith State Park. Waders will be
needed there.

The guides go for the Rogue reel (for their guests) for trolling. The reel will hold 175 yards of backing of 20-pound test line.
The reel has a free spool device and a good drag. But the fly
man would have little, if any, use for a free spool on a fly reel.

Humboldt Bay, off Eureka, California, is another spot for fly-fishing salmon. It is fished off the north jetty from anchored boats. A lead core line is also used here, as in the Smith River. The tackle is similar. The fishing season is in July, according to my reporter—a dedicated fly fisherman and an honest one. He was there around the Fourth of July.

The fly pattern he uses is tied on a Mustad No. 3906, 1/0 hook, a standard-length shank and, what is very interesting, a regular-wire weight. The salmon fly I described for the Smith River is tied on 5 extra-strong wire. How controversial can fly patterns get?

A 3-inch length of silver piping is put on the hook. The way to do this is to shove the eye of the hook into the hollow piping an inch from one end and slide it through the material. Tie it down. This gives about an inch of piping on the hook and a 2-inch extension. Gray squirrel hair is tied in the open end of the piping as a tail. A wing of white polar bear hair is tied in near the eye. On top of this tie is a small amount of green polar bear hair and, on top of the green, a small amount of royal blue polar bear hair. This is what the man said. The flies are used in lengths from 2½ inches to 5 inches, depending on the size of the bait in the bay at fishing time.

CHAPTER 12

Mexico

Prospecting fly fishing in a foreign land is complicated, and Mexico is about as foreign a land to fly fishing as one can find. I did not see one fly fisherman in that part of Mexico I visited. Information on the subject is not available.

In the summer of 1962, having heard of the fantastic fishing in the Gulf of California (Sea of Cortez), I wrote letters. The final result put me on a cabin cruiser in Topolobampo Bay, 13 miles out of Los Mochis. My Mexican guide was not acquainted with fly fishermen. I guess I was the first one he had ever seen.

When in Mexico, do as the Mexicans do. We trolled and caught fish. My Spanish was not good enough, so the guide never got my ideas on fly fishing. I thanked everyone concerned for the trouble and expense, but I realized I would have to go it alone.

I was camped overlooking Topolobampo Bay. The nearby jetty banks were high and difficult to cast from, but I managed to find a few level spots. I picked up sierra and jack crevelle. The early November days were delightful for camping out—no bugs and no cold nights. I found some wading water over soft mud. I missed my pram.

Looking for richer pastures, I headed for Agiabampo Bay, some 30 miles to the north. I got lost on 13 miles of unpaved roads, but the water was finally located. Corvina were abundant. From there I drove to San Carlos, just north of Guaymas. The fishing was terrific. Then to New Kino, west of Hermosilla, with its beaches and rocky points. There I got into sierra and corvina.

Puerto Penasco (rocky point) was my next stop. This fishing village is reached out of Sonoita on Highway 8. It was getting too late in the year—the water was too cold for fly fishing—so after doing some sightseeing, I headed home.

Since fly-fishing information is nonexistent in the area I visited, I considered my prospecting a success. I was satisfied that the potential for good fly fishing was there. In subsequent years, I took 7 month-long camping trips to this area, ranging south to the waters west of Culican.

The trip is not an easy one. Some of the off-the-paved-road fishing spots are hard to find; getting lost is routine. There is the language barrier, especially with some of the Indians who do not understand Spanish. However, I would not miss the experience for all the gold rumored to be in Fort Knox. I've had some unforgettable experiences.

And on to pescado (fish) land . . .

SIERRA MACKEREL. In Mexico this fish is called a sierra. The Latin name is Scomberomorus sierra. I am throwing this in in case you are the scientific type. I could care less about a name. Not too much Latin is spoken today by man or fish.

A sierra is easily recognized. It has a streamlined body with golden dots. The tail is deeply forked, and there are finlets in back of the anal and dorsal fins. It is the only Mexican fish I know of that cuts through a monofilament tippet with the greatest of ease. So if you have your fly cut off, you are in sierra. Sierra only enter shallow water adjacent to deep water. They do not range far up shallow bays.

The sierra is one of the greatest fly rod fish I have encountered anywhere. They hit with express-train speed, are willing strikers, and make long surface runs. They range in size from 16 inches to 26 inches. It is said that they get to be 36 inches long and up to 15 pounds. But I have not seen fish of this size even in commercial nets. The usual size caught is fish enough.

The season for this fishing is from May to November, depending on the fishing grounds. The farther south you fish, the warmer the water. The San Carlos fishing also depends on how much netting is being done. That netting can kill the fly man.

The weather must be considered. It gets awfully hot, even on the beaches, from May to October. And the nights are, at times, uncomfortable for sleeping out. The hot days can be taken if you have air conditioning for cooking and sleeping. It reminds me of the Florida Keys in the summer.

The time of day to fish is the first hours of daylight. The last two hours before dark is second best. From about 9:00 A.M. to 5:00 P.M., the fish go for the siesta bit. Frankly, I think that most of the fish are night feeders.

Last year I received a letter from a friend in Norwood, Pennsylvania. "Sam, make like I am a beginner in the fly fishing game. Give me all the details—a complete picture. I want to get the most out of such a trip as it is a long drive home."

Although I started with an 8-foot Lamiglas blank of stiff action, assembled it (with a cork reel seat), and used it for 5 month-long seasons in Mexico, the 9-foot rod may be more suitable—a choice the fly man will make as an individual. Shooting Heads are best. For those who don't have one, a weight forward tapered line will be needed. The floating type and sinking type are required. The leader, a 9-footer, should taper down to .012 or .0135 inch—the 10- or 12-pound class. Thirty inches is a good tippet length. It will shorten in a hurry if you have more than average "chop-offs."

Whether you use poppers or streamers, sierra have such teeth that the lure loss is very great. When you cast to this fish, if your loss is not more than 50 percent you will be lucky. That is, of course, if you do not use wire. And wire made up of fine strands will not do. It will require single-strand wire. The wire leader subject in relation to fly fishing is complicated. Frankly, I do not know the answer. I just avoid its use.

There seems to be a little more lure loss with poppers than streamers. One morning I watched with dismay as fish, over-sized sierra, hit my poppers and headed for the other side of the gulf. Every popper was bitten off. A dozen poppers long gone.

The streamer fly, tied on a Size 2 or 4, 3 extra-long shank, regular-weight wire hook, of what we can consider a standard pattern, will work in most cases. The streamer should be about 2½ inches over-all. Either bucktail hair or marabou filaments are used. Just remember that the fly loss will be great. I don't fool around. I take 400 hooks (4 boxes) in sizes 2 and 4 and a couple of ounces of marabou plumes (white) and a few white bucktails. I am not joking when I say that if you run out of material a white sheet (if you sleep between sheets) can be used by cutting and tying small strips on the hook. You could resort to that if you run out of regular materials. The poppers are tied on 2s and 4s—the regular humped-shank hooks. All white with a red head.

I make no claims of being a Tommy Edison, but I think I invented an outstanding fly for sharp-toothed fish. I take a 3 extra-long shank hook—a longer shank may be even better—and tie in hair—nothing else—at the bend of the hook. I call it the bare shank fly. It cuts down on sierra loss and is quickly tied. I tie the popper with the cork as far back as possible—a 6 extra-long shank is used for this. It is known as a bare-shank popper. If the fish clamps down on the shank instead of the leader, you are assured of a landed fish.

The usual retrieve is to bring the streamer in with fair speed and the popper in with a retrieve that causes the popper to kick up its heels. But fish can go for the unusual. One October, I was fishing sierra that came by in small schools. I made the usual retrieve, with no results. I knew the fish were feeding by their action in the water. On one cast I got fouled up, and the fly remained in the water with little if any action. That is what the fish wanted, or thought they wanted, and I had a hookup. This fish was landed, and since I was saving fish for a meal, I knocked it over the head to keep it quiet. When I gave it a telling blow, it spewed what looked like white worms—with black eyes—all over the beach. These worms are supposed to be fry and were about 1¼ inches long. A small fly and no retrieve was the answer. I would make as long a cast as possible to reach the feeding fish and then get any slack line back on the reel. During that time the fish took the fly. My conclusion: There was so much bait in the water that a fish was not going to waste time on the chase. Why run for a streetcar if another is stopping at your feet? Evidently the bait did not have the horsepower—the fins— to get away. Frankly, I cannot say just what the bait was. If a fish, it had no fins. If a shrimp, it had no legs. That was the morning that produced 75 strikes in 3 hours—a loss of 50 flies, and 25 fish beached. It was worth the trouble of tying flies all afternoon and on into the night. From a financial standpoint, it meant about $1.50 for hooks and material and less than 4 cents a day for the fishing license.

The water is usually very calm in the early morning, but there is a very small undercurrent close to the beach that stirs up so much sand and gravel that stocking-foot waders are not as practical as boot-foots. Not too much walking is required. I wore the boots even in warm weather. I would suggest carpet or felt soles for all wading, regardless of the bottom. And one should wade out at least far enough for a clear backcast. The water is usually clear enough so no wading staff is needed.

One bit of advice! When wading in quiet water, do not move your feet after a cast. As the line is stripped in, it means a lot of line at your feet. Move your foot and you are stepping on line. You are then in trouble if the fish decides to go places. It will also foul up your next cast. A fishing basket for the stripped-in line may be to your liking but it is not a real necessity. Usually you will not need a landing net, since it is easy to wade the short distance to shore to beach the fish. My article in *Western Outdoors* under the title, "Fly Fishing the Mexican Salt" was written from fishing experienced up to and including 1966. The article was published in December 1967. The fact that commercial fishing started in the fall of '67 put me on the spot. I put in a month of letter-writing getting this fact to the many fly men, and others, who had written for more information on their planned trips to the area. If they had gotten down there and fished San Carlos when the netters were at work, the fly men would have put me in the doghouse.

CORVINA. The corvina is a member of the croaker family. It frequents the warm-water shallows. It looks like an unspotted weakfish (also called sea trout), and the white sea bass, a Pacific croaker. This is the fish that is found in the Salton Sea. However, corvina in the Gulf differ from those in the Salton Sea— they are much easier to catch. Because of the similarity of names, there is confusion between corvina and corbina. The latter is not, to my knowledge, a fly-caught fish.

In the San Carlos area, August—the weather is hot—is the best month for this fishing. Corvina is considered a good food fish. The size range is from a pound to 30.

I have found corvina from Puerto Penasco to Topolobampo. This takes in more than 700 miles of shoreline. Any sandy beach or shallow bay in that area is potential corvina fishing water.

I had heard of Playa de Agiabampo from some unremembered source in 1962. I got fouled up on directions and landed at a wrong arm of the big bay. It was a mullet bay. They were there by the thousands, with dolphins in hot pursuit. One dolphin made a fast U-turn and splashed me good. I realized that I was not in good fishing water, so I drove back to the main highway over 13 miles of unpaved road for better directions. The owner of the motel (now closed down) told me he was going to the fishing bay the next morning and I could follow him. This is the easy way. These unpaved roads do not have signposts, and the usual travel is by the trial-and-error method.

By noon the next day I was camped among a group of un-tenanted grass huts. I was within 30 feet of the water and was 100 yards or so from the small village. I spent the rest of the day getting my tackle ready for the next morning's fishing. I knew from experience that daylight was the prime time.

At the crack of dawn, I got into boot-foots, grabbed my rigged-up rod, and waded out. The rod was an 8-footer as-sembled from a one-piece Lamiglas blank. It was rigged with a floating head, a 20-pound test monofilament shooting line and 200 yards of backing on a large reel, a 9-foot tapered leader with a .012-inch-diameter tippet, and a No. 4 popper, all white with a red head. (See Chapter 8, "Fly-Tying Instructions.")

The wading was on hard sand; the water was calm. There was not a fish in sight. But they were there. The action was fast and furious. I landed corvina up to 24 inches as fast as I could cast, fight the fish, beach, and recast. I knew the Mexicans like corvina, so I kept my catch. I dug a shallow hole in the sand and buried them as protection against the sea gulls. After about 2 hours of this fantastic fishing, it came to a sudden halt. The fish stopped biting or left for deeper water. I cleaned the fish and gave them to villagers. They were tickled pink, and I made friends. After the word got out that I was a fish distributor, there was quite a lineup on the beach. I caught fish in the early-morning hours for a week. The adjacent villagers also got into the act. All I had to do was get the fish up on the sand, and my new friends did the rest. They, in turn, offered tequila—a potent drink, to say the least. I told them in halting Spanish that I had promised my father that I would not touch alcoholic sauce until my 72nd birthday. They accepted my excuse.

Some 30 miles south of Guaymas is the Indian village of Cruz de Piedra (Stone Cross). The beach is 5 miles away as the crow flies, but it seems 20 miles by car, driven by anyone unfamiliar with the criss-cross unpaved roads. (It takes a Christopher Columbus-type fly man to get there.) The beach is several miles long. I camped there for a week. The only persons I saw during my stay were 2 Indian boys who arrived bareback—bareback on a horse. They had a bottle of water (I think it was water), matches, and a couple of handlines. That was their camping equipment. They were going to live on fish, using bait found on the site. They were very curious, and nice kids. The thing that bothered me was their horse. Suppose they did not catch any fish? Maybe the horse was their ace in the hole.

Corvina fishing is blind fishing. They never, to my knowledge, show on the surface, even in very shallow water, so finding them is not easy. But finding them in the early-morning hours results in some fast fishing. The water must be warm for good fishing, which means the fly man will have to put up with some hot summer weather.

I have not mentioned the use of streamers for this fishing. The popper was fished exclusively. It would be very practical if you could fish with another fly man—one using poppers and the other using streamers near the bottom. It could very well work out, with larger fish being caught by the streamer fisherman. In order to do this, you will have to bring the other fly man with you. I do not think you will find one on any of the beaches. I never did.

TRIGGER FISH. The trigger fish is so named because the first of the 3 stout spines of the dorsal fin is locked upright by the second spine when the fish is disturbed. The ones I caught are called the common trigger fish, but they cannot be considered common by the fly man. The largest one in my experience was a large fish, about 18 inches long and 10 inches deep. Fishermen wanted no part of these fish for food until it was discovered they made delicious chowder. Then they were in the kettle.

This is one fish that must be fished with a sinking line—a lead-core head, if you do not object to using it. Or you could use weighted flies on an HiD head. A 2-inch white streamer on a 4 or 6, 3 extra-long shank hook will be suitable. Your usual salt-water fly outfit will be needed. Most of the fishing is from rocky points. Waders are not used, but carpet-soled shoes are.

If there is a special time of day for this fishing, I do not know it. I fish for trigger fish when I have finished with others. I fish after 9 in the morning for them. Since they are tropical fish, summertime should be best. I caught them in October from a rocky point between the San Carlos marina and San Carlos Bay proper. (Calling the open ocean around San Carlos the "bay" is not correct.)

Trigger fish chew up a streamer with ease, but the fight of the fish is compensation. If you can imagine the fight of a 5-pound fresh-water bluegill, you have a comparison.

LADYFISH. One October I was wading about 15 feet off-shore at San Carlos. There was not a fish in sight. But the lady-fish was there. For the next 10 days, they took my Size 4 white popper without hesitation. I had never encountered this fish in the gulf before. And not since. The interesting thing about this fishing is why I did not pick up other salt-water varieties at that time and why ladyfish hit on top when every fishing magazine reader knows they are strictly a bottom-caught fish. Although the proper name for these fish is 10-pounder, the weight is usually 2 or 3 pounds. A 10-pound 10-pounder would be hard to handle. Ladyfish, when hooked, do some interesting bouncing and splashing.

I use a 9-foot tapered leader as a standard, but that is just my opinion. On the popper, a size .011-inch tippet would be suitable. It would also be suitable for a Size 4, 3 extra-long shank, white streamer.

If you start out at daylight fishing the popper and get no results, you might change to a streamer on a sinking head and fish it all the way to the bottom. Without knowing the actual water depth, fish the fly down until it hits bottom, counting all the time. On the next cast, retrieve before the full count. This bottom fishing with a fly is, in my opinion, not very interesting.

Ladyfish are found only in warm water. I have not had enough of this fishing. It is said that night fishing is the time to fish, but ladyfish, at any time or any place, are well worth the fly man's efforts.

COMMON JACK OR CREVELLE. One November day, I was standing on the rocky shore at Topolobampo Bay ready to fish when I saw a small school of fish cruising on the surface some 50 feet away. I made a cast with a Size 4 popper a few feet ahead of them. One fish peeled off and hit the popper hard. I was in business. The fish put up quite a fight. I handled that fish with care. I finally landed a jack some 2 feet long.

After getting a picture, my next thought was to identify the fish. A Mexican told me it was a toro. I know that *toro* means "bull," but that did not help. I asked him if it was a good eating fish, he said, *"Si, señor,"* and I gave it to him. I went back to fishing after patting myself on the back for catching a fish I had never seen before. It was on my first cast of the day.

Naming the fish one catches in Mexico is not easy. This "toro" resembles the common jack or crevelle, but it was a little more slender. Maybe it was thin from hunger. It had a long pectoral fin, the tail was deeply forked, and the head was blunt. So it was a jack or a member of the family. Let's call it a toro when in Mexico and let it go at that.

A .012-inch tippet was used on salt-water fly tackle. Carpet-soled tennis shoes were needed on the wet and slippery rocks.

NEEDLEFISH. The needlefish is related to the flying fish, but the only thing they have in common in an unbalanced tail. They are built like a snake, with long-toothed jaws. They probably average 2 feet long.

I was on the small boat-launching beach at the San Carlos trailer park, looking for sierra activity. There was a disturbance in the water about 100 feet offshore. Since any disturbance in the water is my cup of tea, I got into waders, picked up my rod with its Size 4 popper, and waded out within casting range.

The action came immediately. A fish would strike at the popper half a dozen times before hooking up. At times it hooked itself on the outside of the mouth. The fish went crazy trying to swallow my offering.

This is not a fish one would go out of one's way to fish. It is an available fish, and of some interest, if only for the novelty of hooking one. The fish were, of course, put back without damage. Real fighters, these fish are not. They are strictly a surface fish and so are easy to locate.

PAMPANO. One late October morning, I parked my van off the then unpaved road at San Carlos Bay. It was just light enough to wade out elbow deep in the quiet water. The water was quiet, but the fish were sounding off. I made a cast into a school of fish that was slowly moving out of range. One fish took the popper. By the time I had landed the fish the others were gone.

This was the first fish of its kind I had ever seen, so a picture was in order. After making the numerous necessary adjustments on my camera, I pressed the shutter release, but no click. With 10 rolls of film on hand, the camera would break down on my first picture-taking effort. The fish was 16 inches long and about

10 inches in depth. When I took it to the marina to try to classify it, I was told it was either a world-record pampano or a permit. The permit is similar to a common pampano but much larger.

The fishing called for as long a cast as possible, so the best distance outfit you have should be used. I was fishing a floating head on monofilament shooting line with lots of backing. The Size 4 popper was on the leader—what I call the standard (all white with a red head). The tail can be bucktail hair or marabou fibers. A smaller or a larger popper can also be tried. I stayed with the popper most of the time because almost all the varieties will hit it, and it is more sport. It is possible that if I had used a streamer, I might have had better luck on bigger fish. Who can say?

BICHI. While popper fishing for corvina at Agiabampo, I caught fish that I have not been able to classify. I showed a couple of the fish to a Mexican boy. He spelled out "bichi" on the sand. I took pictures of the fish, and when I returned home, I took the pictures to a famous professor of marine biology at La Jolla's Scripps Institute of Oceanography. He gave me 2 hours of his valuable time. He could not classify the fish. If I had brought the fish, it would have helped, but I ate the evidence on the way home.

A bigger mystery is what gave me the idea that I should try the fish cooked in bacon grease. Now, corvina are supposed to be fine eating, but not for me. But "bichi" are out of this world. I saved every one I caught and really looked forward to eating them.

One morning I saw a dozen bichi on the beach, thrown out by commercial fishermen. Some hogs saw the fish at the same time, but it was no contest. I was wearing waders, which slowed me down. If the fish diet flavored the hogs' meat, I should have eaten the hogs.

The most distinguishing markings on the fish are a deeply forked tail (similar to mackerel) and small finlets in back of the dorsal and anal fins.

The same tackle was used as for corvina—a Size 4 popper. The bichi is similar to corvina in fighting ability—not too spectacular.

Various basses, croakers, snappers, and snook are caught in the warm waters of the Gulf of California.

The bass called a cabrillo is caught over rocky bottom, and a boat of some kind is needed. Some fish are lost in the rocks, but many can be landed by moving the boat directly over the hooked fish and working it loose. The cabrillo I caught were 5-pounders and were good fighters. They reportedly grow much larger.

A sinking head is used. A .012-inch tippet for the 2½-inch marabou fly was suitable for the fish I caught.

I did this fishing in November. The best time of day to fish is early morning before the wind comes up, before the water gets too rough for a small boat.

One of the interesting features of fishing Mexican water is the variety of fish caught. Most of them fell to a popper. At daylight on most bays, fish are abundant and in a mood to grab anything baitlike that moves. If the water is not too deep they will hit on the surface—the only way to fish.

Snook are found at the mouth of Agiabampo Bay and south. Some of the snook holes are hard to locate. I could not find them in Topolobampo Bay in May, but that was my hard luck. They are there. The ocean waters west of Culiacán contain snook, especially at the mouth of the Río San Lorenzo, 40 miles to the south of Culiacán. I would say that fall and late spring would be the time for snook fishing. When the water cools in the winter the snook go deep—or so I am told. You had better check before going after snook. They will take a No. 2 popper or a 3-inch streamer.

Crossing the border into Mexico from the U.S.A. is simple. A tourist card, good for 6 months, is obtained from a Mexican Government Tourist Department office in the United States. It is necessary to fill out a form and show proof of U.S. citizenship. A birth certificate, a voter's registration card, or military discharge papers will be proof. A driver's license will not. A smallpox certificate is no longer needed for re-entry into the United States from Mexico if no other country has been visited during the preceding 14 days. A fishing license is required and is obtained at any Mexican Fish Commission in the United States. It costs $4.00 for a one-month permit and $8.00 for one year. Mexican insurance is a must. This is obtained from your agent or Mexican agencies.

For the fishing area we are concerned with, a motor vehicle permit is issued at Sonoito on Highway 2 or at Nogales on Highway 15. There is no charge for the permit. However, some of the boys may try to collect. The tourist bureau frowns on this. There is also a vehicle inspection—a baggage check, which is simple. Proof of car ownership is needed. There will be one or 2 inspection stops on the way south.

Night driving is not advised because of animals on the unfenced highways. I tried night driving. I saw an oncoming truck with blinking lights and slowed down. There was a horse on the center stripe. Speed limits are a little lower in Mexico and should be followed. In fact, for trouble-free traveling, obey all Mexican rules and regulations. It is the easy way to go.

For tourists from the West Coast, the border can be crossed at Mexicali. I prefer crossing at San Luis, although it is about 30 miles longer. The roads are less confusing there. For other tourists, Nogales may be a better entry point. Both Highway 2 and Highway 15 are good paved roads with little traffic. To me it is a freeway. There are few towns, and even with the slower speed limits, the average speed is good.

Travelers' checks are fine, but Mexican currency is better.

Take enough currency to at least take care of gas and oil. Fifty-peso notes ($4.00) are suggested. Mexican money makes it easy for the service-station operators.

The Mexican Tourist Department patrols Highway 2 and Highway 15 to aid drivers in trouble. They supply some gas, oil, and water, and can perform some mechanical work. They show up every 12 hours or maybe less. Your vehicle should be in top shape before entering Mexico, and it is advisable to carry gas, oil, water, fan belts, etc. My corvan threw a fan belt 50 miles from nowhere, and if I had not taken an extra, I would be there yet. The fisherman who may be miles from a service station should consider tube tires. An extra tube and a tire pump could save the day. I once had 2 flat tubeless tires 50 miles from a service station and almost blew my cool.

Going through Los Mochis to Topolobampo Bay is confusing. Some streets seem to have the right of way but are not so marked. However, the speed limit is very low, so this is not much of a problem.

All government land in Mexico seems to be open for camping. Personally, I have had a lifetime of rough camping. A trailer park with electricity, water, showers, and rest rooms is my idea of living in the great outdoors. There are many such trailer parks. They may get a little crowded during Easter, Labor Day, and over the Christmas holiday. Parks have trailer sections and camping areas. When putting up a tent, supervision is needed, since the underground water pipes may be of plastic and close to the surface. A tent stake could wreak havoc with the water system.

Some campers from the United States think it is dangerous to camp in Mexico. I think it is safer than in the United States. I have been in some lonely spots in Mexico and have had no trouble at all. To me it is a great outdoor country, and the variety of fishing is greater there than in most places in the States. My trips have been solos. Not because I like to fish alone, but it gives fewer problems and more freedom of movement. However, a fishing companion who has the same ideas on fishing as you do would be a pearl beyond price.

Drinking water is a problem. At some trailer parks, trucks come in with bottled water. A deposit on the 5-gallon bottle is required, but the deposit is returned with the empty. The cost of water is low.

There are good grocery stores in the larger towns. But if one has some favorite foods, it is no problem to carry them along. There is no law against going over the border with camping equipment, food, and fishing tackle. As a rule, fish taste like wet paper to me, but some of the Mexican fish are delicious, and I eat fish to make my groceries last longer. Sierra and "bichi" are for me.

Rain can be a problem when driving on unpaved roads. I once came to the town of Guasave, south of Los Mochis, which, because of rain the night before, was slightly under water. I should have turned back, but I had heard of some hot fishing at the mouth of the Sinaloa River. I ended up getting towed out of a newly formed lake in the middle of the road and stayed up on high ground for 2 days until the road dried out. I had a similar experience, during a rain, trying to get to the mouth of Río del Fuertes from Los Mochis. I never reached my destination. The unpaved roads turn into adobe-type mud. These rains are rare in the fall of the year. This is just a warning not to be a brave numbskull. June and July are supposed to be the rainy months.

The natives I met down there were friendly people. I got along in grand style with them. I think that most tourists who get off the beaten path will agree with me. But the tourist who acts as if money grows on trees gives the natives a poor opinion of the North Americans. It could reach the point where they will accept us only for our money.

Recently, I received a call asking about the fishing in the San

Carlos area during the Christmas holidays. The quality of fishing depends on several factors, but mainly on the commercial netting being done at the time. For several years, the small-boat netters have been hitting that water and removing many sierra. They make camp in San Carlos bay right at the fly-fishing hot spot. Their boats and boat traffic ruin fishing. This is a fact but not a complaint. It is their country, and the fish belong to them. The netters are nice people. They had a netful of fish, and they invited me to fish into the haul. I could have snagged a fish on every cast. I had to laugh in spite of the fact that the netters were ruining my fishing.

When I got home, I wrote to the Mexican Tourist Department in Los Angeles to find out what time schedule the netters had so I could plan my trips accordingly. The letter was forwarded to Mexico City. I was told that the netting had no ill effect on sport fishing. I feel that they were making a decision from too great a distance. If they had questioned the motel and trailer park owners, they would have taken an opposite viewpoint.

The other factors that affect the fly fishing are: a drop in water temperature and a lowering thermometer. The fish are tropical, and cooling water, especially, tells them to move to warmer water. The fish head south, and so should the fisherman. One gets into warmer water and weather by moving each hundred miles or so down the boulevard. This past Christmas, some of my fine-feathered friends moved from San Carlos to Topolobampo Bay with good results.

When I look back on 7 month-long trips in Mexico, it is with happy memories. There is such a variety of fish, and everything was, as we Alaskans say, skookum. Good fishing, good camping conditions, good air, and clean water.

It does not seem to take much knowledge of Spanish to get by. I know the few words I really need. Asking about fly fishing in that part of Mexico is a little silly as well as useless. They do not go for this fly-fishing jazz. Truckloads of workmen would stop when I was out in the water fly fishing. But they all cheered. I became famous almost overnight.

The best fishing occurred in October at San Carlos. The days were warm with a few bugs, if a white moth is a bug. The nights were ideal for camping out. Many varieties of fish were available. The fishing was fantastic, especially the popper fishing. May to November is the best time to fish. Not only the days, but the nights are warm.

Sunglasses, sunburn lotion, and mosquito repellent—just in case—should be part of your equipment. The only maps that are of much help are those from auto clubs. The small villages—the starting points for isolated fishing grounds—are shown on these maps, and such a map is definitely needed. The service-station maps just won't do.

Some fine trips could be made with a small boat and kicker. For example, launching a boat at Agiabampo with camping gear, food, and water for a few days' fishing at the estuary—the mouth of the bay—would give great fishing for snook, corvina, bichi, sierra, and others. Late October or early November would be ideal. If you are there at that time, look around for my camp. I just might be there.

CHAPTER 13

Florida

About 20 years ago, I read a magazine article of the wonders of fly fishing in the Florida Keys. It told of such great fishing that I could not stand the pressure. I had to give the fishing the good old college try.

I had received a free Thanksgiving dinner offer from a friend in Atlanta, Georgia. After that dinner, my wife and I headed for the Keys. After getting settled in a nice cabin, with an ocean view, we went prospecting for fish—what else? The scenery was great. The water was there. But where were all the fly fishermen, as advertised in magazine articles? Granted that it was late in the season, but some fish should have been available. Nobody knew a thing about any fishing. After scouting the entire length of the Keys, I knew I was on my own.

Just south of the town of Islamorada, I found a good parking place at the edge of a boat basin. I sat there, wondering why I hadn't taken up golf or polo, when I saw signs of fish. It took little time for me to get with it. The back cast was clear, except for traffic, and I tossed out a streamer and hooked my first snook. I patted myself on the back, landed the snook, and tried for more. I would make a long cast and retrieve all the way in. This resulted in 5 nice snook. They looked nice to me, but I found out later that they were just over the 20-inch limit. But one snook that must have been at least 4 feet long followed my fly. I ran out of retrieve, and the snook almost climbed the bank.

I had a similar experience on a big snook the next day. It looked to be 5 feet long, and again it followed my streamer in to the bank without smashing it. About then I would have liked to have met a fly fisherman who could tell me what I was doing wrong. Maybe I should have been using a large popper to stir that rascal up. I never did find any fly fishermen to teach me the ropes. I did hear a faint murmur somewhere about it not being the right time of the year for bonefish and tarpon.

I made several trips along the Flamingo Road and had some success with baby tarpon and snook. Also, the fishing along the Tamiami Trail was rewarding for small tarpon and snook. I must have established a record of sorts—I drove from Jacksonville to the Florida Keys and back to Tampa and did not see one fly fisherman. That is unbelievable.

We went home. After resting from the 6000-mile drive, I thought maybe the fly men in the Keys might be getting spring fever and would come pouring out from under their rocks. So the first of April found me in a cabin at Laytons on Long Key. I took a small pram along. That April was a good month weatherwise, fishwise, and bugwise. I mean it was a good month for bugs, not for me. The only thing that saved me was a smoke wagon circling the cabins so sleep was possible.

There was a little tidal river on the ocean side, and I would launch the small boat and head down the river for open ocean. The results of this fishing will be told in following stories.

TARPON. A tarpon is similar to an overgrown herring. It also is, in the estimation of many fly men, the greatest fish that swims. It is well named the "silver king." It comes into shallow water and up rivers to feed on smaller fish. Tarpon are found in the warm waters of the Gulf of Mexico, and the Panama Canal Zone, to name two areas.

I have had more fun with tarpon than any other fish I have met. My first experience with these fish—of any size—was in the tidal river I mentioned earlier in this chapter. The month was April—a lovely month, usually, in the Florida Keys. The river was lined with mangroves and was so narrow that it was impossible to cast toward shore. The boat had to be anchored in the middle of this water and the casting made up- or down-river.

I was using a weight forward tapered line and a Size 2 popper with a white body and tail and a red head. It was about 3½ inches over. There wasn't a sign of a fish until the popper hit the water. Tarpon would smash the popper and jump 10 feet into the air. After 2 or 3 jumps, they became very playful. I either got the popper tossed into my face—a handsome face with beautiful brown eyes—or into the highest mangrove branches. At the risk of getting knocked out of my pram, I stayed with the fish for 2 hours. I did not gather one fish. I did gather all the poppers I could reach in the mangroves. Some of my poppers may still be hanging in the high brush. The fish were about 2 feet long. Nothing to brag about.

I do not go along with the assumption that visible tarpon will always cooperate with the fisherman. Henderson Creek, a tidal river located south of Naples on Isle of Capri Road, was loaded with tarpon. They looked to be over 3 feet long—a good size for fly fishing. The fish were 60 feet from my casting position on the bank. There were no back-cast hazards. I threw my popper into that school for hours without a sign of interest by the fish. There were a couple of bait fishermen trying for the fish, but they got no place. I don't know the answer. Maybe a big streamer fished close to the bottom might have worked. A good fly man would have given up with the popper and tried the streamer, and in various sizes as well as water depth. Maybe I missed the boat, and maybe I didn't.

A similar experience happened in some mangrove-lined water

near Collier Seminole State Park. I was in my pram casting 40 feet of line. My popper would hit the tarpon on the head, but I could have had as good results in a casting pool. If mosquitoes had never been born, I would move to the area and find out what is what with tarpon. I do not feel too badly about it since I know a very fine fly man who had the same lack of results on tarpon in Central American water.

BONEFISH. Bonefish, along with tarpon and ladyfish, are similar to the herring. It could be rated with the tarpon as one of the greatest fish that swims. On the incoming tides, it cruises the flats in search of food—flats that are high and dry during low tides. They feed in water barely deep enough to cover them. They are found in warm waters of many lands but became well known in the Florida Keys.

The sport is called bonefishing, but it is more a sport of hunting than fishing. It is done in two ways: The fly man fishes from a boat with a man in the stern poling him over the flats in search of bonefish, or the fly man wades in the shallow water to accomplish the same purpose. The waters of the Keys vary as to the type of bottom. It may be sand, rocks, coral, or impossible-to-wade mud.

The best months for this fishing are April, May, June, and July, with July the least windy and April the best month climate-wise, generally speaking. For the man who has lived in a mild climate—the man who has lived in San Diego within a stone's throw of the ocean—the weather in the favored months is rough. Eating and sleeping under air conditioning is very necessary, but wading in hot weather is not too bad. The wading is done wet, either in short or long trousers and tennis shoes. The wader always air-conditions himself by getting wet.

The wading fly fisherman can get into the hunting act in two ways. The usual method is to enter shallow water on an incoming tide and slowly wade the flats searching for fish, hoping he will see a fish before the fish sees him—and far enough away so that the motion of his casting will not send the fish back to Africa. Keen eyesight and Polaroids mean everything for successful fishing. In shallow wading the flyman, to his disadvantage, is almost fully exposed to the fish.

There is quite a casting problem involved with this type of fishing. You are wading along ready, you hope, to get off a fast cast. And in order to cast, it is necessary to have a certain amount—a certain weight—of line out past the rod tip at all times. The only way to do this that I know of, is to wade along trailing line behind you—enough line so you can make a fast cast with little, if any, false casting. A floating line must be used. The fly seems to ride high enough to keep from getting hooked in the bottom, even in shallow water. If you have trouble in this respect, you can hold the fly in your hand. As a right-hand caster, you will be holding coils of line in your left hand for shooting purposes. You may like a shooting basket for storing this line, but I have never seen one in operation. With 20 feet of trailing line and a 10-foot leader, it will not necessitate holding many coils in your hand.

The casting distance depends, of course, on your ability to sight fish. It may be only 35 feet, or more than 50 feet. If you can spot a bonefish at 50 feet, you have it made. Your rod should be selected with this distance in mind. And while we are on the subject, it has been said that a long rod, as long as $9\frac{1}{2}$ feet, is needed to keep the leader up off the bottom and avoid getting cut off by coral. This may be true. But in my experience (limited, to be sure), the bonefish goes so fast that there is enough tension created to prevent this problem. And so what if you are cut off? If that time should come, it will be after you have had most of your fun. Bonefish usually are not eaten, except by sharks.

Then there is the tailing bonefish (tailers) that puts his face in the mud and his tail above the surface. I refer to this fish as an old man's delight. The old guy can see a tailer, but he could not see a swimming bonefish until he stepped on it. This is my favorite bonefish. It is usually far enough away so I can cast without disturbing the fish. I decide which way it is working and cast about 10 feet in front of its snout. The retrieve is made in 2 ways. One is the steady retrieve, and the other is the stopped retrieve, when you see the fish closing in on your handsome offering. However, please do not ask me to stop retrieving when a good fish is plowing up sand, mud, and water in pursuit of my fly. My nerves would not obey the message from what I refer to as my brain.

One reads of the long runs made by bonefish. I have the opinion, right or wrong, that the length of run depends on how far the fish has to go to get into the depth of water that gives it a feeling of security. There is little doubt in my mind that a bonefish, hooked a mile from deep water, would make an all-out effort to get there. But as to any definite distance, that I cannot say.

As to the fly outfit for bonefishing: The rod and line combination will depend, as noted, on the casting distance you will need. A weight-forward tapered line such as Scientific Anglers, Inc., salt-water type with most of the head weight in the first 25 feet is popular. I would even go for a 20-foot head length. The advantage of a floating line has been noted. The weight of the outfit will not be a consideration. Bonefish are not sighted often enough to make many casts necessary. A tapered leader 10 to 12 feet long is suggested. The tippet should be of the smallest diameter that will turn over the fly you are using.

The bonefish fly has been discussed under fly tying. There is little to add to the discussion. On most salt-water fish, you may get more than one chance at the fish, but this will seldom happen on Mr. Bone. Make sure that your fly is tied so the tail does hang up in the bend of the hook.

Certain other equipment is needed. A long-sleeved lightweight shirt, a wide-brimmed straw hat, Polaroid sunglasses, sun lotion, mosquito repellent, maybe a head net, extra tippets, a fisherman's tool, and a canteen of water may be useful. If you are English, take a couple of tea bags along. After you have been wading awhile under the hot sun, you will find your canteen of water hot enough for Lipton's finest.

My visit to Long Key in April was another prospecting trip. When I hit the open ocean from the tidal river mentioned in the Introduction to Florida fishing, I saw bonefish. I soon found that I needed a poler in my pram to pole me within casting range of the fish. With the boat at anchor, the fish were never feeding into the pram. I had the same trouble when drifting. I tried to wade the water, but it was too deep, and the bottom was mud. The fact that it was windy did not help at all. After a few days of this frustrating fishing with no results, the occupants of the other cabins started to refer to me as that crazy Western cowboy, with remarks that, as a fisherman, I seemed to be mounting my horse from the wrong side. I thought it was about time to give up boating and try wading.

I found a swimming beach on the ocean side of the key. Wearing only shorts and wading shoes, I waded out until I was waist deep. I just stood there. I had heard that bones come in on the tide and cruise close to shore, so I remained in that position—about 70 feet from shore—and watched the water alongshore. Two bonefish came along a few feet from the water's edge, and I tossed my fly about 10 feet in front of them. How simple can fishing be under the right conditions? One took my fly and screamed out of there. I handled that fish with care and finally eased it up on the beach. It looked like a beached whale to me. I immediately took it back to the cabins, to those who had peppered me with snide remarks, to show them what happens when a Western cowboy learns the ropes. I became their hero. My picture was taken, and the Miami *Daily News* gave me a citation. That beautiful fish weighed 7 pounds, 14 ounces.

I had lost a lot of weight from the work and the heat, so when I showed the picture, the comment always was, "Which is the bonefish?"

I must say, I was a little disappointed with the length of this fish's run. It did not go 200 yards in one burst of speed, as advertised. Later, I found out that a bonefish stays in high gear until it reaches deep water, and in this case deep water was not far away.

In 1968, I received an invitation to bonefish out of Key West. The invitation came from a fly man who had had twenty years of this fishing. Arriving on the 28th of May, I found that my new fishing friend was marooned in Yucatan because of stormy weather. I was on my own. I headed for Boco Chico flats. I drove along an ocean road until I found a break in jungle with access to the water. The water was very warm, shallow, and not crystal clear. I had done little wading when I saw a tailer. Checking his feeding direction, I got a good cast off, with the fly landing a few feet in front of the fish. It was a good fish. It came for my fly with terrific speed. Sand and water flew in all directions. I will never know why I did not get a hookup. Maybe I was seen by the fish, and maybe the tail of the fly was out of joint. But to lose the first tailer I ever cast to was disappointing. The way the fish headed out for deep water makes me think I was too visible. I would hate to think that with years of practice, my fly tying was inefficient. I tried 3 more places on this long flat but saw no more tailers. And nontailers would be hard to see in such unclear water. Sharks, yes; bonefish, no.

Getting back to camp, I got out my 40-year-old vise and tied some flies so the material could not possibly foul up in the bend of the hook. I got ready for the next day. Then came the hurricane warning and 3 days of rain. It was so windy that I would have been blown off the water.

My friend got back home shortly thereafter and took me out to a remote key in Florida Bay. We anchored the boat in the shallow water and he, his 13-year-old son, and I went hunting. The water was crystal clear and not over 12 inches deep. I thought I saw a bonefish. After a lot of looking, I decided it was a bone and not more than 30 feet away. I don't know why the fish didn't see me. The fish clobbered my fly. That bonefish had miles to go to reach deep water, and it was getting there with unbelievable speed when the hook pulled out. So I learned one thing too late. I was supposed to put all the strain possible on the leader and sink the barb the second I felt the fish.

While the father was hard at work earning the daily bread, the 13-year-old and I roamed the flats. He was good at the game. And he could see fish with his 20-20 vision. We had no generation gap. He was one of the finest fishing companions I ever met.

Before going on the trip, I read all the fishing stories and looked at all the pictures I could find, but gained little. Fishing with someone in the know is meaningful. Being at the right place at the right time does no harm, either. Throughout this book, I have tried to tell it as it is—the good with the bad. I hope you will learn from both.

ORGANIZATIONS

The San Diego Fly Fishermen's Club is one of the many clubs that has a very efficient method of teaching casting. This club was organized by Charles "Chuck" Elget 10 years ago. Hugh Wright Turner is a well-known member—a former accuracy champion. He was certainly right when he thought up the marabou fly, now widely used with great success on a variety of ocean fish. Chester "Champ" Richards, another member, is a real old-timer at the game—he catches fish with the best of them. Membership has risen from 6 to 80, and this does not take into account the many dropins and dropouts. Since the casting pool is open to the public, many nonmembers have availed themselves of this service.

There is no charge for instructions. However, it would be more practical, maybe, to make a small charge for this very valuable help. As Charlie Chan would say, "No ticket, no laundry." I feel that I should make it clear that Charlie has nothing to do with the actual instructions. However, a fee would have a tendency to weed out the men, women, and children who have Sunday interest in this game and who decide on Monday that they would rather beat up on an innocent little white ball. I believe this is called golf.

No, the best way to start fly fishing is, of course, to buy this book. The reader can then make up his mind as to his interest. And without interest, the road will be rough. This is true whether you are flying a kite or landing on the moon with a homemade rocket strapped on your back. Instructors are happy if their customers go ape for the game.

The *Salt Water Fly Rodders of America, International,* was organized in New Jersey several years ago to help those interested in this sport. It now has chapters in many states. Fred Schrier, chairman of its Executive Committee, told me the organization is showing a good growth pattern. It has more than 3000 members. The SWFRA has an advisory board made up of many experts. On the West Coast, such fly-fishing experts as Jim Green, a former world-distance champion; Myron Gregory, considered to be at the top of the class in knowledge of casting; Larry Green, the writer, and Jon Tarantino, present world champion, are board members.

The *Federation of Fly Fishermen is a Great Organization,* with many members, member clubs, and affiliates. The FFF covers most of the states and, like other fishing clubs, is dedicated to fly fishing, associated activities, conservation, and good fellowship. J. Stanley Lloyd, chairman of the Southern Council, sent me the following list of member clubs as of June 3, 1971:

Andover Fly Fishers, Massachusetts
Anglers' Club of Chicago, Illinois
Anglers' Club of Portland, Oregon
Arizona Fly Casters, Phoenix
Bea-Moc Rod & Gun Club, Roscoe, New York
Beaverkill Fly Fishers, Roscoe, New York
Blue Dun Anglers, Medford, Massachusetts
Boise Valley Fly Fishermen, Idaho
California Fly Fishermen, Sacramento
Cascade Fly Fishing Club, Washington
Castle Creek Fishing Club, Corning, New York
Clearwater Fly Casters, Washington
Connecticut Fly Fishermen's Assoc.
Desert Fly Casters, Mesa, Arizona
Diablo Valley Flyfishermen, California
Evergreen Fly Fishing Club, Washington
Fly Casters of Boulder, Colorado
Flycasters, Inc., Campbell, California
Fly Fishermen for Conservation, California
Fly Fishers Club, Orange County, California
Fontinalis Fly Fishermen, New York
Golden Gate Angling & Casting, California
Green Country Fly Fishers, Oklahoma
Henryville Conservation Club, New York
Indianapolis Fly Casters, Indiana
Inglewood Fly Fishermen, California
Inland Empire Fly Fishing Club, Washington

Joe Jefferson Club, Inc., New Jersey
Kittitas Valley Fly Casters, Washington
Livermore Fly Fishermen, California
Long Beach Casting Club, California
Long Beach Women's Casting Club, California
Lower Columbia Flyfishers, Washington
McKenzie Fly Fishers, Oregon
Montreal Anglers & Hunters, Quebec, Canada
Napa Valley Fly Fishermen, California
North Coast Fly Fishermen, California
Oakland Casting Club, California
Olympic Fly Fishers, Edmonds, Washington
Palm Springs Rod & Gun Club, California
Palo Alto Fly Fishers, California
Pasadena Casting Club, California
Potomac Valley Fly Fishermen, Maryland
Prairie Fly Fishers, Oklahoma
Puget Sound Fly Fishing Club, Washington
Putnam Trout Association, New York
Rhody Fly Rodders, Providence, Rhode Island
Salinas Valley Fly Fishermen, California
"Salty" Fly Rodders of New York, New York
San Diego Fly Fishermen, California
Southwest Montana Fly Fishermen
Stanislaus Fly Fishermen, California
The Steamboaters, Oregon
Theodore Gordon Fly Fishers, New York
Totem Fly Fishers, Vancouver, British Columbia, Canada
United Fly Tyers, Massachusetts
Upper Fishing Creek Fly Fishers, Pennsylvania
Waders of the Wolf, Wisconsin
Washington Fly Fishing Club, Seattle
Wilderness Fly Fishers, California
Wyndham Angler's Club, New Zealand
Zanesfield Rod and Gun Club, Ohio
Klamath Country Fly Casters, Oregon
Rogue Flyfishers, Oregon

Sun Valley Flyfishers, Idaho
Susquehannock Fly Fishers, Pennsylvania
Wasatch Fly Casters, Salt Lake City, Utah

To get in touch with any of these clubs, call your recreation department or local newspaper's sports department or write to Membership Service Office, Federation of Fly Fishermen, 15513 Haas Avenue, Gardena, California 90249.